THROUGH DARK PLACES: TRUE STORIES OF HUMAN TRAGEDY, FAITH, AND MIRACLES

by Sid Baron

DEAR ELLEN,
THIS BOOK IS A GIFT FROM YOUR DAD. THE FIRST CHAPTER WILL MAKE YOU GRATEFUL THAT HE IS STILL LIVING. SAME FOR YOUR UNCLE JOHN.
GOD BLESS YOU AND YOUR FAMILY

Sid Baron
2011

Through Dark Places
True stories of Human Tragedy, Faith and Miracles

Published by:
Exxel Publishing Co.
323 Telegraph Rd.
Bellingham, WA 98226
Tel.: 360-671-2275
Toll free: 1-877-939-1999

Ordering information:
You can order today and you need not pay until after you receive the book (s.) An invoice payable by personal check or Credit Card will be enclosed with your order.

Visit www.sidbaron.com for easy on-line ordering.
Contact author via E-mail: sietze@msn.com

Mail your order to:
Exxel Publishing Co.
323 Telegraph Rd.
Bellingham, WA 98226

$19.95 plus $2.95 postage (Canada $3.95)
Inquire about quantity discounts.

Ordering by telephone or fax:
Telephone: 360-671-2275
Toll free: 1-877-939-1999
Fax: 360-671-7616

ISBN 978-0-9703469-1-9

Author's Note

Each chapter in this book stands alone as a nonfiction account of an extraordinary event in the lives of ordinary people. Extraordinary events have always intrigued me, whether they are tragic or inspirational. I hope my readers will enjoy them and be blessed by them, as I have.

Three of the poignant stories in this volume were written by (my brother) Henry Baron. Henry J. Baron is Professor of English, Emeritus, at Calvin College in Grand Rapids, Michigan, and has long been active as a writer, editor, and translator.

Table of Contents

Guardian Angels

Sid rushed to answer the phone, scooping the wireless unit off its cradle. He had not yet put in his hearing aids for the day and had probably missed several rings. "Hello," he said breathlessly.

The cheerful voice of his son Jim greeted him. "Dad, today's the Fourth of July, and you haven't had a ride in my new nineteen-foot outboard boat. Why don't you join me and Gerald for a ride in Bellingham Harbor?"

Sid turned to the window and saw that the sun shone brightly. The sky was clear. "That's right, it's a national holiday. Our offices will be closed, and I can't think of any holiday activity that could possibly beat your invitation."

After completing the arrangements, he replaced the telephone. Even before the receiver had settled into the cradle, a thought began to form in his mind. He sat down at the kitchen table and stared out through the sliding glass door, where a woodpecker was gorging itself on the hanging basket of suet. After every two or three vigorous pecks into the suet, the bird would stop and observe its territory.

It must be very safety-conscious, he thought. *If sudden danger should threaten, it wants to make sure that it has an escape plan and route.*

Sid stared out across the small lake. A mother duck was escorting eight ducklings near the shore, looking out for her babies' safety. Undoubtedly, she would be prepared to protect and defend her young with her life. It seemed that all of God's creatures had been given an innate sense of self-protection and responsibility to protect the lives of loved ones, or even strangers.

As he contemplated the upcoming boat ride around the harbor, a million memories floated to the surface of his mind. He recalled fun-filled moments from the annual family vacation at nearby Wildwood Resort, and precious times spent with Jim, Gerald, and his other children. As he began sifting through the memories, he realized that each represented a moment in time, like a photograph, ready to appear when called upon. Some were so vivid and clear, it was as if they had happened yesterday. Some were painful, others pleasant. The most overpowering of them, though, was the memory of a fearful day more than forty years earlier, when he had almost lost everything.

He thought of the plaque on the wall of his childhood home. He could not remember the precise wording on the plaque, but it went something like this: *The fear of impending peril is often greater than the peril feared. But should the peril overtake us, God will always be close.*

He knew why the terrifying memory had surfaced. The plans for today's pleasurable experience would take him near to that place where the memory had been formed all those years ago. Whenever it surfaced, his inner being still experienced aftershocks.

~~~

When Sid arrived at the dock where the boat would be launched, his two oldest sons were already busy loosening the various straps that tied the boat securely to its trailer. Jim, tall and slender, approached him with a wide smile and slapped him on the back. Ger, with his glasses and well-trimmed beard, waved from his position at the boat. Both had inherited
~~~

the blue eyes that ran in the Baron family.

Climbing into the pickup truck, Jim slowly backed the trailer onto the downward-sloping launch platform and into the water. When Gerald gave the signal that the back end of the boat was partially submerged, Jim stopped the pickup. The rest of the launching operation was done manually, and after Sid had boarded, taking the passenger seat, the boat slid smoothly into the waters of Bellingham Bay in Puget Sound.

The channel leading to the deeper water of the bay was sheltered from times of storm by a long wall of rockery. A long line of large black seabirds occupied the top of the wall. Their heads held high, they acted like alert sentinels, looking left and right as if doing mandatory guard duty. Unlike the noisy seagulls swooping over their formation along the top of the seawall, they remained silent as they watched the boat slowly approaching deep waters.

Jim turned in the pilot seat. “You want to pilot this ship, Dad?”

“Why don’t you and Ger sit up front?” Sid suggested. “I’ll sit back here and just watch the beauty of the scenery.”

Gerald moved to the co-pilot seat next to his brother.

“Where would you like to go?” Jim asked.

Sid pointed to the southern tip of Lummi Island. “Maybe in that direction first, and then cut across and return along the hillside coastline. Will that work?”

“Sure, starting near where Skagit County becomes Whatcom County?”

Sid nodded in agreement and settled into the comfortable seat behind his two oldest sons.

He looked at them with pride. They, together with their four siblings, were all grown now. The carefree years of youth, of fun and laughter, of playing hide and seek or bicycle races with them, were merely memories of a distant past. Now they and three of their siblings were parents of grown children themselves. They had already proven by the conduct of their lives to be successful parents and contributing, God-fearing citizens.

The boat turned away from the shores of Lummi Island and moved toward the Whatcom County shoreline, visible in the distance. There, the hills rose several hundred feet above sea level. As the boat neared the shoreline, Sid looked intently at the rocky hill rising above the waterline.

Now close to shore and to the railroad tracks at the foot of the shoreline, the boat turned toward Bellingham. Deep in reverie, Sid stared at the craggy hillside. The boat made a turn in a northwesterly heading, and suddenly he saw the narrow rock-and-concrete roadway, rising about six feet above the water, with railroad tracks connecting Bellingham to the shoreline across the bay inlet.

He had flown over this site hundreds of times while on final approach to the Bellingham airport. This was the first time he had seen it from sea level.

"Bring the boat to a stop here, boys," he called out.

His mind and stomach were churning. He broke out in a cold sweat as his eyes traced a path from his current location to the mainland of Bellingham and the house that stood on the first hilltop, several hundred feet above sea level.

He looked at the house again, looked at its chimney. The antenna that had once been attached to it was gone.

An aftershock of memories struck him again, shaking him to the core.

~~~

On a lazy summer morning forty years earlier, he stood just outside his family's vacation cabin, watching his boys toss a football back and forth. His two beautiful, blond, blue-eyed little girls were already busying themselves for a day of fun in the wading area near the shallow shore of the big lake.

He heard someone yelling his name and looked in their direction. It was the wife of the crusty resort owner. She motioned for him to come. "Someone wants to speak to you on the phone," she yelled.
~~~

He hurried to the little store and picked up the receiver from the counter.

"Hi, Sid," greeted his friend Herm. "I know you're enjoying your annual four-day vacation at Wildwood, but an important client has requested a meeting, and it could mean a good sale."

Sid knew that Herm's industry, chick hatcheries, was in a period of recession and consolidation. The big were getting bigger, and the small operators were gradually being squeezed into economic oblivion.

"The problem is, this client lives in Chehalis," Herm went on. "That's a four-hour drive. With your airplane, you could get me there in probably under an hour. I hate to pull you away from your family vacation, but it would sure save a lot of time if you could fly me there." He sounded reluctant to ask the favor.

Herm was a big, outgoing man you could not dislike. With an easy smile and a firm handshake, he was always ready to help others. Sid had no problem doing the favor and agreed to meet him at the Bellingham airport a little before eleven. Herm would call his potential client and ask him to meet over lunch at the Chehalis airport.

When Sid arrived at the airport, Herm had already warmed the airplane. He had a student pilot rating and was familiar with the craft. He had invited his good friend and brother-in-law John along for the ride.

Soon, all three were strapped into the Piper Tripacer. Sid taxied to the departure end of the runway and performed the pre-takeoff checks, which were simple enough on a non-complex airplane like the Tripacer. In no time, it had broken the bonds of earth and become airborne. With three adult men, the small airplane was close to maximum weight as defined in the plane's operating handbook. With no headphones or intercom system in the airplane, conversation without shouting was not possible. They settled in for the hour-long flight to Chehalis.

Sid was not familiar with the Chehalis airport and consulted his Washington State airport guidebook. It covered all the details such as runway length, runway elevation above sea level, and runway direction. They were at an altitude of 3,000 feet when arriving above the airport. He checked the windsock on the field and determined that the wind was from the south. This meant that they would land on runway 180, directly into the wind. The airport did not have a control tower. It simply had a designated communication frequency, which all aircraft in the vicinity were required to use to announce their position, altitude, direction of flight, and detailed position reports when intending to land.

Sid announced his position and intention to descend to traffic pattern altitude of 1,200 feet. The landing was smooth, and they quickly taxied to the base operations office, which also featured a coffee shop.

Immediately upon exiting the aircraft, they were approached by two official-looking men. One showed his credentials as an FAA inspector. “May I see your pilot license and current medical certificate?” the inspector said.

This had never happened before. Sid handed over the documents and glanced at Herm and John silently. Nothing aboard the aircraft had been out of the ordinary, and he assumed it was just a random inspection.

The inspector returned the documents. “Did any of you see another aircraft?” he asked.

They shook their heads. In spite of the fact that all three of them had been looking, no one had seen or heard anything on the frequency.

The FAA officials looked at each other.

“Both of us were absolutely sure that you were about to collide with another aircraft,” the inspector said. “From our vantage point, it appeared unavoidable. We fully expected to have the debris and bodies from two aircraft raining down on the airport.” The northbound aircraft, he explained, was a faster, low-wing model. Meanwhile, Sid’s was a high-wing

Tripacer.

Sid was sobered by the information. By the somber faces of his companions, he knew they were, too.

~~~

A little after two o'clock in the afternoon, when Herm had finished his meeting, they headed northbound, back to Bellingham. They climbed to 3,000 feet. Aided by a tailwind, Sid calculated that groundspeed was close to 150 miles per hour. Filtered by a layer of high clouds, the sun no longer shone brightly. As they droned along, the thickening clouds soon obscured the sun altogether.

The weather didn't become a concern until they approached Paine Field in Everett. They were now skirting the bottom of a cloud layer. The first raindrops pelted noisily against the windshield.

Becoming worried, Sid reduced power and descended to 2,000 feet. He checked the remaining fuel indicator. He guessed that there would be sufficient fuel to make it to Bellingham, but not much, if any, to spare. In his mind, a pilot running out of fuel was never excusable. The accident reports he had read indicated that fuel starvation was a frequent cause of accidents. Most of those resulted in off-airport emergency landings, not always successful and often resulting in the loss of lives.

"I think we'll stop at Arlington for some fuel," he told Herm. "Considering the deteriorating weather conditions, especially toward the north, let's get a weather report for the airport in Bellingham."

~~~

While the attendant filled both wing tanks, Sid went into the operations office, where the fuel bill would be paid. More important at the moment was the availability of a telephone. He would be able to call the Bellingham flight service station to inquire about weather conditions at the airport.

The office was tiny and somewhat cluttered, with small displays of aviation charts, books, headphones, and other flying-related items. A few model airplanes dangled from the ceiling.

The same young man who had fueled the Tripacer now moved behind the counter.

"Can I use your telephone for a call to Bellingham?" Sid asked him. "The weather is deteriorating. It doesn't look good from the air looking toward the north. It's worth a long-distance call. Better safe than sorry," he added, almost as an afterthought.

Two men sitting at the coffee counter nearby heard the conversation. The older of the two, probably still in his mid-twenties, piped up immediately. "I just came from Bellingham with my student pilot. It wasn't beautiful, but good enough for flying under Visual Flight Rules."

Sid listened attentively. This was a flight instructor who had just come from where they were headed. How could any information be more accurate or up-to-date?

The flight instructor continued, "I'm going the have my student do a couple of touch-and-goes at Skagit Regional Airport in Burlington, and then head right back to Bellingham."

Sid thanked him, his mind now at ease. After paying the fuel bill, he looked at Herm and John, who had come out of the rain to join him in the office.

"Okay, guys, no more worries about running out of fuel," he said as he led them back outside. "If we don't hoist her back into the air soon, they'll probably beat us back to Bellingham." He gestured to the flight instructor and his student.

When departing Arlington, Sid knew they wouldn't be able to climb to 3,000 feet. Still, he was surprised when, already at 1,500 feet of altitude, the lower clouds momentarily enveloped them. He wasted no time in lowering the nose of the airplane, forcing it to lose altitude. He was not qualified to fly in clouds and rely solely on instruments to keep the aircraft right-side-up. He knew that inadvertently flying into clouds by pilots who were qualified to fly only under Visual Flight Rules almost always resulted in the pilot losing control, and the inevitable crashes were nearly always fatal.

Just north of Stanwood, he reluctantly reduced altitude to 1,000 feet. The weather ahead did not appear encouraging. He banked the airplane slightly to the left to look at the weather behind them. With concern, he noted that it was also closing in rapidly. They could still safely turn around and make it back to Arlington. If he hadn't heard the flight instructor say that the weather to Bellingham was not a problem, that was exactly what he would have done: return to the Arlington airport. Instead, he pushed on.

By the time he left the Skagit County shoreline behind and headed across the bay into Bellingham, they were down to 500 feet. Looking ahead, he grew tense. The clouds appeared to have settled on top of the waves. Heavy rain further reduced visibility to practically zero.

It was imperative that he maintain some ground reference. He turned toward the hills until they were visible directly off the right wing of the airplane. Holding his breath, he slowed the speed to about 75 miles per hour.

With anxiety and fear multiplying exponentially, he noticed that his altitude had dropped to ten feet above sea level. They were simply skimming the waves just below the wheels, very close to the hillside.

John sat quietly in the backseat. Undoubtedly, he was fully aware of the hazards that surrounded the airplane. Meanwhile, Herm practically had his nose against the windshield, intently looking ahead.

Suddenly, with a loud, terrified voice, Herm yelled, "Pull up!"

Even though Sid didn't see the obstruction dead ahead, there was no time to ask questions.

Simultaneously, he pushed in the carburetor icing and throttle to their stops and briskly pulled back on the control yoke, raising the nose of the airplane. The Tripacer immediately responded and began to climb at just above stall speed.

A railroad trestle passed directly beneath them, missing the airplane by mere feet.

As they became lost in the clouds, Sid heard a slight thump. A quick glance out of the left window told him that his left landing wheel was turning. He caught a glimpse of a disintegrating TV antenna. They had just missed a house on the hilltop, invisible in the fog, and had caught the antenna with the wheel.

With heart pounding, Sid kept climbing into the clouds.

He concentrated on his turn and bank indicator to keep the wings level. His ground-school pilot training had taught him never to panic but to keep flying the airplane.

Time seemed to stand still. He did not know whether minutes or seconds passed before they broke out of the clouds into brilliant sunlight. Instantly, he saw the Bellingham airport in the distance.

Minutes later, the Tripacer landed safely on the runway, and Sid taxied to their tie-down position, his hands shaking on the controls.

As the three of them climbed out of the airplane, his friends' faces were white and somber. They exchanged no conversation. The nervous tension would not release them. They had narrowly missed death.

Afterward, more slowly than normal, Sid traversed the winding roads leading to the resort. The spasms and involuntary shaking seemed to emanate from deep within his being.

That Piper Tripacer could not have climbed that steeply, he thought, *especially because there was no excess speed available to allow the airplane to zoom. It was fully loaded with fuel and three grown men.*

Baffled, he shook his head. He could hardly believe that he was alive, or that he would have the chance to hold his children in his arms again.

~~~

The memory faded, and Sid once again drifted with his two sons in the waters of Bellingham Bay. He wiped the sweat from his face and took deep breaths, trying to clear his mind of the terror he had relived. But the lump in his throat remained.

Later that afternoon, driving home along Guide Meridian Road, he knew his longtime wife, Margaret, would want to know all the details of a marvelous boat ride with their two oldest sons. He realized with a searing sense of guilt that he had never told her about the event that had nearly ripped their lives apart. She hadn't been happy when he agreed to fly Herm to Chehalis instead of enjoying the day with the family. He had by no means wanted to tell her how close he had come to never seeing them again.

He couldn't bring himself to do so now. He couldn't tell her that he hadn't been very good company during the boat ride, or that an event from long ago had kept his mind captive even before the ride started. The ride had turned into a journey of introspection and self-discovery, and he wasn't finished yet.

Impulsively, he pulled the car into a used car lot. Using his cell phone, he dialed his home phone number. Margaret answered, and after some small talk about a wonderful afternoon, he told her that he would be home a little late. He knew that she wouldn't let him go without wanting to know the details of his extra activities, so he quickly fabricated an excuse, saying he needed to stop at the office and take care of a few things.

As he ended the call and turned south once again on Guide Meridian Road, he hoped she wouldn't try to call him at the office. He wouldn't be there.

Instead, he turned off the long, winding road into Wildwood Resort on the shores of Lake Whatcom. Still gripped by his recollections of that day, he felt compelled to visit the place where he had almost left his family for good.
~~~

Parking in the guest area under the large oak trees, he strolled over to the dock, where fishermen launched their boats.

Now the family memories of so many years ago didn't just float to the surface; they exploded with crystal-clear vividness, as if time had stood still. The small fishing boat on the water reminded him of Grandpa Tjoelker, Margaret's father, returning with his two oldest grandsons, Jim and Jerry, after hours of fishing. The boys enjoyed fishing with Grandpa, but the length of his fishing outings had increasingly tested their endurance as they grew older.

Sid turned on the dock and began laughing involuntarily. It was as if a movie had begun to play in his mind. There they were: his son Ron, the tallest and strongest of the four brothers, and his twelve-year-old cousin Ray. Previously, Sid had made arrangements with Ron to help him pull a prank on Ray.

"Hey, Ray," Ron called out to his cousin, who promptly came running, his blond hair flapping in the breeze. "You want to make an easy hundred dollars?"

Ray's eyes lit up and opened wide. "Sure, but what do I have to do?"

Ron was quick to respond. "You don't really have to do anything. You can't lose. It's a one-way bet. See, we're standing on this dock . . ."

Ray nodded at the obvious.

"So here's the deal: if we can't throw you at least thirty feet into the lake off this dock, then you get a one-hundred-dollar bill."

Ray crossed his arms. "How far is thirty feet?" he asked.

Ron took ten long steps on the dock. "That's close to thirty feet."

Ray glanced at the distance and said, "I weigh more than a hundred pounds. You guys can never throw me that far."

"Well, Ray, give us a chance, and if we give up, you

get a hundred dollars."

Ray was mentally already counting his winnings when Ron and Sid picked him up by the feet and shoulders. A couple of swings later, he went sailing – except gravity took over, and he dropped like a sack of chicken scratch straight into the water.

He sputtered mightily as he climbed triumphantly onto the dock to claim the prize. Immediately, Ron and Sid picked him up again, and after another mighty heave, he plopped into the cold water of Lake Whatcom. Again he surfaced and was immediately apprehended for another toss, with the assertion that the second toss was better than the first. They were clearly making headway. They assured him that after a few more mighty practice tosses, they would make it to thirty feet. They just had to be given a chance.

Shaking like a leaf on a stormy day, Ray had had enough and escaped to his cabin to warm up.

~~~

Now, still standing on the dock, Sid turned and looked in the direction of the cabins. They appeared as they had many years before, the day he had returned from his near-fatal flight. He and his family had stayed in the third cabin from the left for a number of years while enjoying their annual vacation. It was quite a party, eagerly awaited by the family members, which included grandparents and at least one of Margaret's sisters with her family.

Everywhere he looked, the scenery evoked fresh memories. He strolled across the old rickety bridge that crossed a creek. At this time of the year, it was always dry. He came to the campground, dotted with numerous three-wheelers, motor homes, and tents. A garbage can was still tied to a large oak tree.

A fond smile once again moderated the serious expression on his face. He recalled Joe Burns, the owner of the campgrounds. Far from sophisticated, Joe was a cursing, heavy-drinking, rough and tough character.
~~~

"That damn bear was here again last night," Joe had griped early one morning. He ranted and raved about the indescribable mess the bear had left throughout the campgrounds. "Garbage everywhere," he said, sprinkling his tiradc liberally with unprintable language.

Ron heard the same story from the tough-talking owner. That evening, Ron showed up with a very authentic-looking bear suit. Under cover of darkness, he climbed into his suit and waddled through the campgrounds, visiting garbage cans and scattering people who had congregated around campsites.

Unfortunately for Ron, someone quickly notified Joe Burns of the bear's presence. Swearing and cursing powerfully, Joe came racing across the old wooden bridge, shotgun at the ready.

Ron raised his paws in total surrender and yelled, "Don't shoot! Don't shoot!"

Now, as Sid strolled through the resort, more memories of pleasant scenes appeared everywhere: playing toddlers; kids and adults competing at volleyball; family dinners around a huge picnic table on the lawn near the cabin. If the Tripacer had struck the trestle, or the house with its antenna, none of these memories would have happened. His wife and children would have had to make new memories without him.

An involuntary spasm struck him – another aftershock of fear from that unforgettable day so long ago.

He leaned against a gnarled oak tree as his eyes blurred with tears. His throat constricted. He knew he shouldn't be here; he shouldn't be able to recall these vacations with his beloved family. Earlier today, he had seen the spot where three bodies should have been found.

What happened there shouldn't have been possible, he thought once again. After all these years, the realization came to him like lightning: *It was a miracle.*

He had a guardian angel. No, he had a host of guardian angels.

It was a miracle!

He climbed into his car. He wanted to see his wife, to tell her, finally, of the intervention that had saved his life and the lives of his two friends. As he guided the car toward home, the pent-up tensions begged for release.

Lifting his eyes to the sky, he involuntarily screamed, "Thank you, God! Thank you."

It Will Never Go Away

Zach's fishing pole lay on the bottom of the rowboat. He looked at the un-baited hook. The oars hung idle, one on each side of the small boat. He looked at the placid waters of Lake Riley. Except for a few silky streaks of high cirrus clouds, the sky was blue. Slowly turning his head, he gazed at the mountains that seemed to surround Lake Riley. Lush carpets of green grass graced the mountainsides. The tranquility of the scene and the majestic splendor of the scenery could not possibly be lost on him as he sat on the bench in the little rowboat. His gaze came to rest on nearby Ebey Mountain, which rose grandly nearly 1,800 feet above sea level.

As he stared at the serene sight of Ebey Mountain, it was as if an explosion of memories were triggered. He lowered his head, dabbed at his eyes, and no longer noticed the unused fishing pole lying in the boat or the oars hanging uselessly on the sides. With amazing clarity, a scene unfolded before his closed eyes.

~~~

His father sat on the front bench of the boat. His eight-year-old brother, Lee, sat on the left, and five-year-old Zach on the right. Each held a fishing pole. With an excited whoop, Lee yelled, "I got one!" as he grabbed a firmer hold on his fishing pole and began to reel in his catch.
~~~

"Keep the tip of your pole down," said their father, Lee Sr. "Looks like you might have caught a big one. Don't let him get away."

Young Lee was a bundle of concentration. As the boy continued reeling, the fish came suddenly into view. It was a good-sized trout.

"Keep the tip of the pole down," Dad reminded him, eager to give his oldest son a hand. "I'll get the net and help get that puppy in the boat."

Lee kept his fishing pole low as he reeled in the rest of the line. The fish was now clearly visible as it struggled wildly, trying to break its connection with the hook. Their father carefully placed his net below the squirming fish and deftly lifted it into the boat.

"Golly, Lee," Dad said admiringly, "I think you just caught the biggest trout in the lake."

Quickly the hook was re-baited, and Lee was fishing again. Almost immediately, he yelled, "I got another one. Wow, this one is strong! This is a real fighter, Dad."

Lee Sr. picked up the net again as he watched his son expertly reel in the fighting fish, all the while keeping his pole down.

Just before Lee's second catch was safely in the net, Zach's pole began jerking. "Hey, Dad, I've got one, too," Zach said. "Can you reel it in for me?" He was younger than his brother and wanted to be certain that his catch wouldn't get away.

"Sure, Zach. No problem." Lee Sr. finished putting away the second big trout his oldest son had caught and took the pole from Zach. "Okay, I'll show you how to do it." He kept reeling, and soon the fish came into view. "I'll get it very close to the boat so you can grab it," he said. "Those buggers are slippery, so hold 'im tight."

Zach grabbed the little trout and looked at his dad.

He shook his head. "Sorry, Zach. That one's too small. Just unhook it and toss it in again."

That was the way it went all afternoon. While his big brother was catching three more big ones, Zach caught two more little ones. He wasn't really jealous of his brother, but he wasn't proud of himself, either.

As they headed for the shore at the end of their fishing expedition, Zach said to his big brother, "Lee, next time will you let me sit on the side of the boat where you were sitting?"

"Sure," said Lee, "but why?"

"The big fish in the lake were all on your side of the boat."

Lee draped his arm around his little brother's shoulder, nodded agreeably, and smiled.

~~~

Zach awoke from his reverie and brushed moisture from his eyes with the back of his hands. He looked around. His boat had drifted clear across the lake, but he hadn't noticed. *How long has it been?* he asked himself. He picked up the oars from the bottom of the boat and began rowing; steering in the direction where he had launched what seemed like just moments ago. His strong arms rowed swiftly and steadily. A half hour later, he docked where he had started.

After securing the boat, he stood on the shore and once more looked out across Lake Riley. The memories of the past would not release him. Abruptly, he turned and headed for his car. An inner force seemed to propel him, and when he drove away, he didn't even have to think about which roads to take. It was as if his car were on autopilot. All the roads looked strangely familiar, even though he hadn't been here for many years.

He stopped at what looked like a small, unpainted shack. This was the home where all his memories of a happy childhood had been formed. After a fishing outing with his dad and brother Lee, they would always return to this house. Here they would join his mother, his younger brother Jacob, his sister Bernadette, and baby sister Jennifer. He could still see his dad and grandpa digging day after day under the house
~~~

to create space for a basement and a couple of extra bedrooms. Grandpa and Grandma lived next door.

He climbed out of the car and gazed at the house. It was much as he remembered it. Strangers now lived inside.

A smile crossed his face as he remembered the many Sundays after attending church that the whole family would go to Grandma's house next door for dinner. Grandma was a petite, attractive Filipino lady with dark hair, friendly brown eyes, and an easy smile. Grandpa had met her when he served in the armed forces during the Second World War. Sunday afternoon, with up to fourteen people around the dinner table at Grandma's house, was a feast. There were uncles and aunts and at least three cousins. Grandma would prepare delicious meals. Zach's favorite was *dinuguan*, a popular dish in the Philippines featuring a combination of rice, meats, and vegetables. He sat next to his brother Lee while everyone enjoyed Grandma's special dessert of mini-donuts generously sprinkled with sugar. Uncles and aunts would tell about their naughtiness during childhood.

A smile returned to his face as he remembered the fun, laughter, and family togetherness during those wonderful get-togethers at Grandma's house. Still facing the house, he lowered himself and sat on his heels. While memories cascaded through his head, he plucked a dandelion flower and studied it.

Life is like a fragile blooming flower, he thought. *When the storm comes, its stem breaks. Its beauty is lost. Its life is gone. No one remembers the place where once it bloomed.*

Gently he laid the flower on the ground and rose to his feet. The dandelion had given rise to another memory. Lifting his eyes to Ebey Mountain, he began climbing. All the while, he searched intently among the trees and the mountain's forestation. Suddenly, his breath caught as his searching eyes found the object he was looking for. He quickened his pace, moving low-hanging branches out of his path as the slope increased and his breathing became labored.

When he reached the white cross, he fell to his knees. He remembered the day his father had placed it there. He stared at it silently as tears mingled with perspiration on his face.

In the distance, he saw his car, parked close to the little house were he had grown up. He realized how weary he was. He was no longer the youngster with boundless energy who had grown up with his loving family in the little house. Moving through the trees, he found a grassy area to rest where he could still see the old family home and the nearby home where his grandparents had lived.

Images and memories paraded through his mind in endless procession.

~~~

He and his brother were playing hide and seek.

Lee will never find me, he thought, as he lay quietly in a very narrow space between a mound of dirt and the house.

"That's clever, Zach," exclaimed eight-year-old Lee, "but I found you!" Lee appeared over his hiding space, his dark hair mussed and his brown eyes wide with delight.

Zach got up and brushed the sand off his clothes before sitting down on the grass next to Lee.

They looked up at the growing pile of dirt.

"Man, Dad and Grandpa have really been digging under the house," said Lee. "This pile is twice as high as it was last week. Even Mom is working on it. She's loading dirt in the wheelbarrow and starting another pile and putting some of it in that little ditch. She's wearing a belt below her big stomach." Lee looked over at him. "You know why they're doing that, Zach?" he asked, nuzzling close to his brother's ear so he could be heard whispering.

"No. Why are they?"

"You know, Mom is going to have another baby. That's why her stomach is so big."

Zach listened with rapt attention as Lee continued.
~~~

"They're hauling out all the dirt from underneath the house so Dad and Grandpa can build a couple more bedrooms."

"Cool," responded Zach. "Maybe you and I will get a new bedroom."

Suddenly there was a tap on the window.

"Look – Dad wants us to come in," Lee said. "He's sitting at his easel, painting those pretty pictures."

Zach glanced up and saw his father beckoning them inside. With his wavy dark hair and moustache, Zach thought his father looked like an older, bigger version of his brother Lee. Maybe that was why they shared the same name.

Jumping up, Lee grabbed Zach's hand, and together they raced to the front door. They rushed into the small room where their father sat, looking with satisfaction at his latest nearly completed work of art.

Zach stood on one side of their father, and Lee on the other, each resting an arm on one of his shoulders. They gazed at the two birds in the painting, with the lake in the background surrounded by hills and trees.

"Dad, it's beautiful," Lee exclaimed. "The birds seem to be looking right at us. Are you going to sell the painting?"

Putting his arms around his sons, he said, "No, boys, I don't do it for money. I do it because I love painting pictures of God's fantastic creation. I can worship the Creator while I paint the landscape and some of His creatures." He paused for a few moments and squeezed them tightly. "I've got a happy surprise for you, boys."

"What are we going to do?" Zack asked with excitement.

"First we're going to the Forest Park Animal Farm in Everett. You can ride ponies and play with other farm animals. Then we're going to Lake Riley to catch a few fish."

"Wow, Dad, that's cool!" they both exclaimed.

"Don't you have to work tomorrow?" Lee asked.

"Well, yes. My new wallboard installation business is

taking off pretty good. My friend Rick Lange is going to work for me tomorrow. You know, he's the tall guy who plays guitar. He's an artist on the guitar like I'm an artist with the paintbrush. Neither of us makes any money with our art. But he wants work to earn some extra money because his wife is expecting their first baby. I know school is starting again next week, so I wanted to spend a fun day with my two oldest boys."

Their father hugged them again while they gave each other high fives.

~~~

With a clarity that amazed him, Zach remembered that beautiful day and all the fun things they had done. He remembered how much he had loved the two Lees in his life, his dad and his eight-year-old brother. He knew that the bond of love could never be broken.

He had his own family now, and he was creating memories with his own children.

Still deep in his reverie, he jumped as the stillness exploded with a flash of lightning, immediately followed by a blast of thunder that reverberated from the hillsides all around. He hadn't noticed the skies darkening and the ominous clouds forming to the west. Now, together with the thunder and lightning, it didn't just start raining – it poured.

No one looking at him would have noticed the tears mingling with the rainwater that poured down his face.

This must be a cloudburst, he thought. He'd read about cloudbursts but never experienced one. Frantically, he looked for shelter. *Not under a large tree*, he told himself. A large tree was a perfect target for a lightning strike. Instead, he spotted some thick undergrowth nearby and crawled deep into the thick bushes. They provided some shelter from the heavy rain.

As quickly as the storm had unleashed its lightning, thunder, and water, the sun shone again. The storm clouds moved across the sky toward the mountains in the east.
~~~

Crawling out of his shelter, Zachary spotted his car in the distance near the foot of the mountain and raced down the mountainside toward it. Opening the door, breathing heavily after the downhill race, he slid behind the steering wheel. His clothes were wet, but he barely noticed.

He stared at the small, dilapidated house where all his memories had originated. He felt a twinge of anger mixed with sadness. He didn't want to give in to the memories that beckoned him to return to a time long past. But they resurfaced again with such clarity that he knew they would never fade.

~~~

In the car on their way back from the Everett Animal Farm, Zach gave his brother a playful slap on the shoulder and asked, "What did you do to the pony you were riding this morning?"

"Man," said Lee, "I think that pony was old and cranky. It tried to knock me off by kicking its hind legs up in the air."

"He did throw you off, but you landed on your feet."

"No, Zach," Lee said emphatically, "that stupid thing was trying to throw me off, but I jumped off before it succeeded. And when I got off, it tried to kick me and bite me. I'm telling ya, Lee, that stupid thing was really mean."

Arriving at home after the incredible day spent with Dad, the boys bounded out of the car as soon as he put it in park, and they made a beeline for the house to tell Mom all about their day. Nearly at the front door, they heard a car horn. They stopped and looked.

It was Rick Lange, the family friend who had worked that day to keep one of their father's customers happy. Rick was just returning from the customer's house. He wore his usual overalls, and his shoulder-length brown hair was neatly combed.

"Hey, good to see you, Rick," their father called out. "How did the job go today?"
~~~

"Man, I've got you one happy customer, buddy. They paid me cash for the whole job." With that, he pulled a wad of bills from his pocket and handed the money to Lee Sr., who counted the currency and handed a number of bills back to Rick.

Rick looked at the bills, and after counting, said, "No, that's too much, Lee."

Lee Sr. cut him off. "Listen, Rick, because you were willing to pinch-hit for me, I had a fantastic day with my two oldest boys. They will remember and talk about it for the rest of their lives. I appreciate it more than the wages I just paid you. Say hello to your wife. By the way, when do you expect her to present you with a little baby?"

Rick's face brightened with a wide smile. "Early November. That'll really be somethin'. I'm excited already." He shook their father's hand and turned toward Lee and Zach. "Hey, kids, come here." He walked the four paces to his pickup truck and pulled his guitar from the seat. "I want to play and sing for you guys. Is that okay?"

Zach and his brother gathered around.

Rick placed the guitar strap around his left shoulder, plucked a few cords, paused, and then started playing and singing:

"Jesus loves the little children.
All the children of the world.
Red and yellow, black and white
All are precious in his sight.
Jesus loves the children of the world."

They stood there silently, mouths open. "T-that was b-beautiful," stammered Lee. Zach nodded his head.

Rick gave them an affectionate tap on top of their heads and turned to their father. "Thanks, buddy. See ya soon," he said, and drove away.

~~~
~~~

After supper that evening, the telephone rang. Lee Sr. picked it up. He said, “Hello,” then listened intently and remained silent. That was unusual. As Zach watched his dad’s face, Zach could tell he was getting some very sad information. Finally, with his voice breaking, he said, “I’m sorry, Jenny . . . I’m so sorry.” With that, he replaced the telephone on its cradle, sat down in his chair, and lowered his head, covering his face with both hands. His body shook with spasms of emotion.

Mom got up from her chair and put baby Jennifer on the couch. Quickly she moved to her husband. “What happened, Lee? What happened?”

It seemed like long moments before he raised his head and looked at his wife. His voice choking with emotion, he stammered, “Rick . . . is dead.”

They were all speechless. Other than Zach’s grandpa, who lived next door, Rick was Dad’s best friend.

On his way home to his wife in Everett, Rick had stopped at a tavern. He had become intoxicated and was killed instantly when his car slammed into a tree. Jenny had suddenly become a young widow. Rick would never see his unborn child. He would never feel his child’s little arms around his neck or hear the whisper in his ears, “I love you, Daddy.”

~~~

On Christmas Eve, 1978, Zach’s family drove to the home of Rick Lange’s young widow and her baby. Full of excitement, they piled into the family van. Lee was eight, Zach was six, Bernadette was seven, Jacob three, and then there was little baby Jennifer. The kids spent a fun evening at Jenny’s home. After Rick’s death Jenny had no means of income and was very poor. The DeBerry family had gathered enough money to surprise Jenny with a little baby crib as a Christmas present. Surely the joy of Christmas was sobered for the adults because of the recent loss of Rick’s life.

Finally, the family had a picture taken gathered around
~~~

the Christmas tree, and then it was time to climb into the van again for the ride home. Dad was driving. Mom, holding baby Jennifer, sat in the backseat with Aunt Lynda, who was living with them.

In no time, the kids were fast asleep. Lee and Zach, sitting in the front seat, leaned against each other and were soon in deep slumber.

They were headed north on Highway 9, back to their little home in Arlington. That's when their world exploded.

Their lives changed forever.

An intoxicated driver, behind the wheel of a Volkswagen Beetle, ran a stop sign and slammed into their van, flipping it onto its side.

The impact was so strong that Zach and his brother Lee were ejected from the vehicle, crashing through the windshield. His brother Jacob and sister Bernadette were also ejected. Jacob and Bernadette ended up in the middle of Highway 9, still in their sleeping bags. Their mother Judy flew from the rear of the van, with baby Jennifer still in her arms.

There were few seatbelts in 1978, but their father and Aunt Lynda somehow remained in the van during the carnage.

Zach woke up in a ditch. Several people stood around him, talking and asking if they should move him or leave him there. Someone covered him with a blanket or jacket to keep him warm. He heard people screaming, yelling, crying. He heard sirens. A policeman was screaming into his radio.

The injuries Zach sustained from being ejected through the windshield were major. The loss of blood from deep cuts on his head caused him to black out.

He woke again in the ambulance and looked over to his side. Next to him lay his brother Lee. Zach could see only blood.

Once again, he blacked out.

The family was transported to Providence General

Hospital. Zach's brother Jacob remembered seeing Zach being rolled along on a gurney, covered with blood, only the whites of his eyes visible. Bernadette and Jacob were placed on an examination table. Across the room, their mom and dad lay on another table. Everyone was crying.

Zach remained in the hospital for six weeks. His head was shaved, revealing the many cuts. Doctors were concerned about possible brain injuries and put him through many tests. The trauma left him with seizure problems that would plague him for years.

~~~

Taking one last look at the house where he had grown up, Zach started his car and drove to the nearby cemetery, where he parked at the entrance. Again deep in thought, he slowly walked among the marble headstones and monuments. His thoughts drifted back to the day he'd been released from Providence General Hospital. He remembered coming home.

~~~

The day he was discharged, his father and his brother Jacob arrived at the hospital to pick him up. His face was still swollen from his injuries, but he was so excited to go home and be with his family again. Finally, he was home!

As he walked through the house, he knew something wasn't right. Where was his older brother, Lee?

He was greeted by his sister and younger brother, and then he noticed the Christmas tree still up, with presents still underneath, as if Christmas hadn't passed yet.

"Why is the tree still up?" he asked his mother. "Whose presents are those under the tree?"

Mom took his hand and walked him over to the dining table. Teary-eyed, she said, "Zach, I'm so sorry to have to tell you, but your brother Lee didn't survive. He broke his neck and died on impact."

Zach sat at the table, speechless. His mother hugged him and held him as an avalanche of thoughts tumbled through his mind.

His big brother and best friend was gone!

They would never play together again. They would never see each other again. Not during his lifetime.

Lee would never grow up.

He was gone forever.

~~~

Walking among the gravestones, the pain of grief Zach still felt was numbing. It was excruciating.

He stopped and looked at the small marble stone right in front of him. He stared at it and read:

OUR SON
Lee Roy DeBerry Jr.
Nov. 19, 1970 – Dec. 24, 1978

He kneeled as tears filled his eyes. Below this gravestone were the remains of his beloved brother. Spontaneously, he spoke in a whisper:

"Brother, I was so looking forward to seeing you when I finally came out of the hospital. I was inconsolable when Mom told me you were already here. I didn't even know about your funeral.

"I still miss you every day. I know you're in heaven. Maybe you can hear me, maybe not. Maybe you know what happened to our loving little family after we were hit by a drunk driver and you were killed. But you may not know, because there is no pain and sadness in heaven.

"Lee, I'm not little anymore. I have my own family now. I named my oldest son after you and after our dad. Someday I'll join you with all the redeemed through all the ages of time, and we'll rejoice in the beautiful palaces of God's eternal kingdom for all eternity."

Slowly he walked away from his brother's gravesite. He stopped and looked across the large cemetery. *There must be thousands of graves*, he judged, by the many flat-lying headstones and monuments of every size and description. His
~~~

thoughts returned to the time following his brother's death.

~~~

Even as a small boy, Zach knew that their family would never be the same. They had all lost an irreplaceable loved one. That aching void could never bc filled.

Zach became quiet and kept to himself. He spent a lot of time staring out the window, and when he went outside to the places where he had once played with his brother, he was always by himself. Quite some time passed before Zach finally started playing again. He was also teased at school for the beanie hat he wore to cover his shaven head and deep scars. Classmates would rip it off his head and laugh.

Meanwhile, their father had lost his oldest, namesake son. It affected him more deeply than they were able to understand as children.

Nobody in the family talked about their feelings. It was a quiet, sad time for them all. Their mother spent many sleepless, crying nights.

No one involved with the collision had insurance. The hospital bills were insurmountable. For months, the family tried to find a way to survive. They couldn't. Zach's parents had to go through bankruptcy. Lee Sr. lost his business.

Then, less than two years after losing his son, Lee Sr. had to absorb another shock when his father suddenly died. Grandpa and Grandma DeBerry lived right next door. Grandpa had helped Lee dig the basement and add two more bedrooms. Lee and his father were best friends. He had been a corporal in the U.S. Army, serving in Korea. He was only in his late fifties.

Lee Sr. was devastated. It was a heavier blow than he was able to bear. This loving husband and father turned to alcohol. How ironic that he would turn to the very substance that had brought their family all these adversities!

Filled with alcohol, this loving man became destructive and abusive. The man they loved and adored became a stranger they feared intensely.
~~~

Zach's mother began getting phone calls from the Arlington Police Department, saying, "Come pick up your husband." Usually, he had passed out somewhere or had gotten into a bar fight. Sometimes he would be gone for days at a time, and the family would have no food in the house.

At times, for a few days, he once again became the kind, loving father they knew. There would be family outings. He would take Zach fishing or riding in his boat. He would play with the kids and have a good time. Zach and his younger siblings were hopeful that they could be a happy family again. But no matter how hard their father tried, the demons of alcoholism would not release him. This once loving father and husband was transformed by the insidious power of alcohol.

Zach's mother threatened to leave. His father fell deeper into depression and alcoholism.

Never would Zach forget seeing his father next to the McDonald's off Broadway in Everett. Mom and the kids were walking. Their father was drunk and crying. He yelled to his wife, "I'm going to get help, Judy." He waved a piece of paper with the telephone number of a rehabilitation facility. "I'm going to get help. I can't live without you and the kids."

Their mother had heard too many good intentions too often.

Their father drove away, crying . . . crying about losing his oldest namesake son, his father, his business, and now his family.

He didn't want to be the man he had become.

~~~

Suddenly, Zach saw it. Another headstone.

He kneeled and read:

Lee Roy DeBerry
Sp.4 U.S. Army
Vietnam
March 30, 1947 – April 27, 1983
~~~

It was a long time ago, Dad, he said silently. *I'm almost the same age now as you were when you were buried here. I'm so sorry that you couldn't break the power alcohol had over you.*

His father had parked close to the school. Zach's cousin was the first to see the car and found Lee sitting in the front seat, a Bible and a small cross necklace lying on his chest. Pictures of every member of their family had been pasted to the dashboard. He had died by inhaling carbon monoxide.

His battle with death, loss, bankruptcy, and alcoholism was over.

I still love you, Dad. It will never go away.

~~~

Her name was Jody. She was not an alcoholic. She had gone to a Christmas party with family members. Someone had mixed juices with whiskey. Jody may not have known what she was drinking at the time.

On her way home, her VW Bug crashed violently into the DeBerrys' van when she failed to see a stop sign.

Jody was injured and also taken to Providence General Hospital in Everett. She was very concerned about the occupants of the demolished van. Her parents told her that the whole family had been taken to the hospital. Jody felt totally responsible, knowing that the collision was her fault. She didn't know yet that it had been deadly. Her parents didn't want to tell her about the death of eight-year-old Lee DeBerry.

Not long after she was released from the hospital, she learned the awful truth. She was inconsolable. Now she knew that her actions had resulted in the death of a little boy.

Was that a burden she would have to live with the rest of her life? No, it was too heavy to bear.

She would never drink and drive again.

Jody killed herself.
~~~

She was only twenty years old.
It will never go away!

Epilogue

Zachary DeBerry lives in Lynden, Washington. He is married and they have three teen-aged children; two sons and one daughter. At his place of employment he is known as "Zach of all trades". He earned that reputation because of his unique ability to "pinch hit" in every department of the business where he is employed.

The tragic memories of his youth often haunt him and cause periods of depression. He knows that his late father knew and believed in his Savior. He understands that, as an imperfect human being, his dad was unable to cope with the losses he had suffered. Zach does not want to dwell on the times his dad came home as an intoxicated monster when every member of the family feared and felt his actions and presence. He wants to remember his dad as the sensitive, artistic, hard working loving father he was before the ravages of life's experiences changed him and Zach's life and his family forever. He knows that the memories of the tragedies in his life will never go away but reiterates: "I still love my dad".

(To contact Zach Deberry, e-mail: zachdeb@hotmail.com)

The Longest Week . . . and Beyond

Sid walked up the stairs and opened the door to his daughter's room. A tidal wave of recollections rushed through the doorway toward him.

The beautifully decorated bedroom was nearly empty now. His wife had a great talent for decorating, and he admired the pale green theme of the bedroom that had been occupied by their younger daughter. Julie had since gone on to college and married. He stared at the lazily moving mobiles hanging from the ceiling, depicting the graceful motion of nature and his daughter's life. And there, carefully attached to the wall, was the motto Julie lived by: *Let everything that has breath praise the Lord.*

These represented the sentimental keepsakes of a young girl's life. He remembered staring at the slowly rotating mobiles while he searched for inspiration and imagination to come up with a fresh "Joany Jones" bedtime story for his little daughters. He had tiptoed in often late at night to plant a kiss on a sleeping forehead framed by golden curls.

As a little girl clutching her "blankie," it was Julie who had stood on the sidewalk in front of the family home, looking along the sidewalk of Front Street, until she recognized the man walking from his store on his way home. It was her daddy. Racing as fast as her little legs could carry her, she fell into his outstretched arms. He hoisted her onto his shoulders for a "horsey back ride" home.

It was Julie who tugged and pulled until she had a chair near the front door. When it was time for her older brothers to leave for school, she would climb on top of the chair. She didn't want her brothers to leave for the whole day without a goodbye kiss.

It was Julie he had watched intently while videotaping her high school track final competition at Mount Baker High School. Her legs were pumping. Only one competitor remained ahead of her, only one girl to beat. During the final quarter lap, Julie summoned all her reserves and won the race in record time. She collapsed into her older sister's waiting arms.

Once more, Sid looked at the empty room, the empty bed, the barely moving mobiles, the white FM-AM clock radio.

A tear trickled down his cheek. Fear, anxiety, and deep concern weighed heavily on his shoulders.

~~~

The previous day had been a long one at the office. Mondays were usually extra busy. When he had arrived home in the evening, he found a red Subaru parked near the back door. It belonged to Julie.

Pulling his car into the garage, he entered the house. His petite daughter stood by the door as if waiting for him, her sparkling eyes wide with excitement. She gave him a hug and said, "Daddy, I have a surprise for you. I'm going to have a baby!"

"Wow, congratulations, sweetheart!" he said, hugging her again, this time even more tightly.

He learned that she had come from her job in Lynnwood to have dinner with her mother. During dinner, she had made the surprise announcement.

Looking at his wife Margaret's glowing face, he knew she couldn't be happier. All four of Julie's older brothers
~~~

were married and had children. He knew how much she loved their grandchildren, as he did. Julie's older sister was not married. It was very special for them to have a daughter who was expecting a baby.

Returning to their seats at the dinner table, Julie and Margaret continued their animated mother-daughter conversation for a short time before Julie returned home. The red Subaru slowly disappeared down the long driveway before she turned south on Guide Meridian Road to return to her husband and their home in Snohomish County.

Sid went to bed about 11:30 and, using the remote control, turned on the bedroom TV. Margaret joined him soon afterward. Faintly, he heard the ringing of a telephone. Margaret's hearing was better, and both listened intently.

"It must be in the TV studio of the program," she said.

"Must have been," he responded as he clicked the *mute* button on the remote. "Although it seems strange that there would be a ringing telephone in the studio while a one-on-one interview is going on."

Click. The TV sound returned, and the program continued until midnight.

Later, as he lay in bed, drifting into slumber, he heard the sound of the locked front door opening. Alarmed, he bumped his wife. Both instantly became wide awake. He was more alarmed still when he heard footsteps approaching the bedroom.

Out of the dark came a familiar voice. "Hey, Mom and Dad. It's me, Alan."

He groped for the light switch. There stood their youngest son, Alan, his face pale and very serious.

"What is it, Alan?" Margaret asked with alarm.

"Bad news," he said.

Instantly, Sid and Margaret both sat up straight in bed. Almost in unison came the question: "What happened?"

With a pained look, Alan replied, "Julie was in a wreck."

Sid grasped Margaret's hand on top of the bedsheet.

Again, in unison came the question: "Bad?"

Alan nodded and looked down at the floor, as if he could not bear the burden of his news. "She was hit by a drunk driver."

Sid took his wife's hand again, not daring to ask the question: *Is she alive?* Fearing the worst, he struggled with this shocking new reality that had just exploded their quiet night and peaceful lives with dramatic swiftness.

Alan still stared at the floor, no doubt fighting his own emotions as his mind flooded with memories of his younger sister. Then he looked up and answered the question that, while unasked, had been hanging in the air like a large black cloud. "She's unconscious. She's in the critical care unit at Everett General Hospital."

Praying silently, Sid scrambled out of bed with his wife and dressed in record time. Minutes later, the three were on their way to Everett, an hour's drive south of their home in northern Washington State. There was virtually no traffic at that early-morning hour. There was little conversation as Sid drove, struggling with the unthinkable but real possibility that he might not see his daughter alive.

Finally, Margaret broke the silence. "We have often talked about our blessings," she said. Sid nodded in agreement as she continued. "We know so many people who've lost a child or a grandchild and experienced sorrows and tragedy."

At least a full minute passed before he responded. He knew what his wife said was true, but that didn't make what had happened to Julie now "right."

"Yes, you're right, hon," he said before another minute of pondering. "I know that God didn't promise that our pathway would always be a flowery bed of ease without pain along the way. But I can't accept that somehow it's fair and just that it should now be our turn." Feebly, he attempted to comfort his wife.

There was no further conversation. Sid increased the speed to slightly over 80 miles per hour. They raced through the Marysville area. He silently struggled with one haunting question: *Is she still alive?* Silently, he prayed. He was sure his wife and son did the same.

He pulled the car into the parking lot of Everett General Hospital. Before turning off the ignition, he glanced at the digital clock. It read 2:23 a.m.

He spotted their oldest son Jim waiting in the parking area, anticipating their arrival. Jim also lived in Snohomish County and had arrived at the hospital first. His dark hair was mussed, his eyes wide with worry.

Reluctantly, Sid climbed out of the car, filled with the fear that they would soon have to deal with that great, unalterable reality of death.

Meanwhile, Margaret burst from the car and embraced her firstborn son. "Jim, is she still alive?" she asked with a quavering but urgent voice.

"She's alive but unconscious," he said, his voice heavy.

Instantly, their spirits were lifted.

"Where there's life, there's hope," Margaret said, grabbing Sid's arm tightly.

As they walked through the long hospital corridor, Sid silently repeated his prayer of gratitude over and over.

They took the elevator to the third floor and found the waiting room of the critical care unit. Most family members were already gathered there. There were hugs and weak smiles on tear-stained faces.

Their son Alan pointed to the large window separating the waiting room from the corridor. "There she is. There's Julie."

They all craned their necks to look. Then Sid saw her. Strapped to a gurney, she was being wheeled from X-ray back to her room in the CCU. She looked so normal, with no external sign of any injuries. No cuts, no bleeding, no large bandages. She appeared so normal– except that she didn't look back at them. She didn't smile. She didn't wave. Sid knew she would have, had she been conscious. Her eyes remained closed.

He stared through the window even after the gurney had disappeared from view. *Just unconscious*, he reminded himself. *She just has to wake up, certainly by morning.*

They walked into the lobby of the Everett Pacific Hotel at about 4:00 a.m. A clerk appeared from an inner office. He looked surprised. "Just for tonight?" he asked.

"We don't know how long we'll be staying," Margaret said in a tired voice. "Our daughter Julie was hit by a drunk driver and is in the hospital. She's in a coma."

The young man's eyes widened. He introduced himself. "My name is Mark," he said. "I worked as a paramedic on the scene. It took us a long time to remove her from the vehicle. It didn't look good. We were afraid she might have a broken neck and handled her very carefully. She was non-responsive. I was worried about her."

Sid nodded. "We're worried, too."

"Please keep me informed about her condition," Mark said. "I know my fellow paramedics were all worried, too, and I'll give them updates."

"Do you know anything about the drunk driver?" Sid asked.

Mark nodded somberly. "He was also injured and was taken to the same hospital in a different ambulance."

"Were his injuries serious?"

"No. He was able to walk on his own, but he wasn't very steady. His speech was slurred, and he told us that he lived in his old car."

Grateful for the information, they went to bed. Sid prayed until restless slumber claimed him for only a short time. When he awoke, Margaret was already gone. Gone to the hospital, he knew. He would just call the hospital and get confirmation of his soul's sincere desire, for Julie to be wide awake and on the road to recovery.

He called the hospital and asked for the desk nurse in the critical care department. The phone rang repeatedly with no response. His mind drifted to an earlier time when his oldest son, Jim, had fallen from a haymow while helping his brother-in-law during a busy haying season.

"Critical care unit." The voice startled him.

"Hello, this is Julie's father. How is she this morning?"

"She had a restless night."

"Is she conscious?" he asked.

"Oh, no. She's in a deep coma."

He felt punctured and instantly engulfed by fear and anxiety. Searching for some foundation for hope, he asked, "How is she doing?"

"She's very restless. She has serious closed-head injuries. Her heart rate is dangerously high. We're watching her closely."

He dared ask no more.

His son Jim picked him up at the hotel. Together they walked into the hospital and up to the waiting room on the third floor.

As he entered Julie's room, he found his daughter thrashing around restlessly in the bed. Thick restraints held her arms to prevent her from pulling out the various tubes inserted into her body. Even though she was in a deep coma, her flailing arms and tortured facial expression indicated that she was experiencing incredible pain. Her heart raced dangerously.

Frightened, he sat down at her side and laid a hand gently on her arm.

On various occasions, he had read that people in a coma were often keenly aware of their environment and, while unable to respond, might hear conversation. The family had actually been advised to talk to Julie with reassuring optimism. If that might help, he would certainly do his share.

Repeatedly, he told her that she had hardly been injured in the rear-end collision. "You just need to wake up, honey," he said. "And you know, Julie, even your baby is okay. They took pictures. I saw them. They know it's a little boy, and the embryo is not injured. I have the picture right here in my wallet."

Julie gave no indication that she understood. She continued to struggle silently, her eyes clenched tightly shut. He used dozens of tissues to remove the foam from her mouth. The fear that she might not survive weighed enormously on him.

When two nurses entered the room, he left and joined the many family members already gathered in the waiting room.

Julie's sister, Kay Lynn, had to be called. Only a week earlier, she had left for New York to begin a new job. Now she received the shocking news that her only sister was in critical condition in Everett General Hospital. Immediately, she made arrangements to return to Seattle on the first available flight.

Just after ten o'clock in the evening, she arrived at the hospital. Sid hugged his older daughter and accompanied her into Julie's room. He had failed to prepare her for the sight of Julie's restless agony, and she broke down in uncontrollable sobs when she saw her sister.

Now his six children were all at the hospital. Together, they prayed for Julie's recovery, besieging the Almighty to spare her life.

Often, fear pressed upon him with paralyzing intensity. As the hours turned into days, with no change in Julie's condition, his faith was frequently assaulted by anxiety. He so desperately wanted to hear an encouraging prognosis.

One afternoon, while he and Margaret were leaving Julie's room to join their other children, they saw Dr. Wright, Julie's neurosurgeon, approaching. They peppered him with questions.

His responses were carefully guarded. Dr. Wright

clearly didn't want to give the family false hope. "Closed-head injuries usually are caused by a violent concussion, coupled with a contra-concussion," he explained. "Such violent head trauma usually causes massive brain damage."

Sid nodded somberly. "We understand that Julie might have serious residual deficiencies," he said, "but we're so grateful her life was spared."

"You cannot assume her life will be spared," the doctor responded instantly and firmly. "Her blood pressure and heart rate are dangerously high and can result in sudden brain hemorrhage and death. As long as she remains in the critical care unit, her condition will remain life-threatening."

A deep gloom settled over them. The glimmers of optimism they had felt only minutes earlier were suddenly dimmed.

Later, as Sid walked to their room along the corridor of the hotel, the lights of his optimism weren't just dimmed by tear-filled eyes and a fear-filled heart; they were totally extinguished.

~~~

When morning dawned, the night's restless slumber had not lessened his gloom.

He walked into Julie's room. He watched her heart rate on the monitor. It was very high. Even though she received sedation, she seemed restless and in pain.

He dabbed the foam from her mouth. He prayed quietly and said loving and encouraging words to his daughter. She gave no indication that she heard. Inside, he screamed. Julie couldn't see the tears.

An hour later, he was driving north on I-5 to his office in Bellingham. Now he didn't have to hide the tears. He didn't have to talk to God silently. He could even talk to Julie. He was alone.

Julie, when Mom was expecting you, I was distressed. Our business was nearly broke. Bankruptcy was looming darkly. How could I possibly provide for such a large family?
~~~

And now with another one on the way, there would be one more mouth to feed. Where was the next paycheck coming from?

"Oh God," he cried aloud, "You aren't going to take her now because I didn't want her then, are You?"

He remembered picking up his little infant daughter from her crib while her mother had gone to church. He had looked into her sky-blue eyes and suddenly known how much he loved this precious child. He had promised her then that, with God's help, he would work even harder to provide for her, her sister, and her four brothers. He had promised her that he would be the best daddy any little girl could ever have.

He often listened to the 200-voice Scottish male choir on his car tape player. He enjoyed singing along with the familiar hymns he'd learned so long ago, and they would lift his spirits.

Jesus Savior, pilot me
Over life's tempestuous sea;
Unknown waves before me roll.
Hiding rocks and treacherous shoal;
Chart and compass come from Thee,
Jesus Savior pilot me.

Nothing lifted his spirits now. He prayed silently, *Oh Lord, you know Julie's life always was an inspiration. Her heart was always filled with care, concern, and compassion for the less fortunate. Lord, please don't take her life now. You know she will continue to live an exemplary life of service in Your kingdom here on earth. Allow her to give life to the new embryonic life she is carrying in her body. Please, Lord, don't take her now.*

~~~

A few hours later, he flew his Cessna Skylane back to Everett, landing at Paine Field. He quickly drove to the hospital, only to discover that there had been no change in Julie's
~~~

condition. As he ate dinner with his wife and loved ones, they exchanged little conversation. The mood was somber. The gloom of fear and uncertainty weighed heavily on each one of them.

After dinner, all went to room 443 in the CCU. All watched the agonized expression on Julie's beautiful face. With tear-streaked cheeks, they hugged each other. Those embraces reflected so clearly the strong bonds of love they felt for each other, their hopes, their faith, and their fears.

Never had the family been more aware of the tenuousness, fragility, and preciousness of life. An extraordinary event had happened, deeply affecting them. Nothing in life could have prepared them for coping with the life-threatening injury of a beloved child. There was no escape from the pain and the dread.

~~~

Later that evening, exactly one week after the dreadful collision, Sid found himself alone in the waiting room.

He walked outside, into the dark evening. The words from the Scottish male choir floated through his head:

Beyond the sunset,
Oh glad reunion
With our dear loved ones
Who've gone before . . .

Anger gripped him in the solitude of the night. Silently, he screamed toward the dark heavens, *Oh Lord, that is no comfort now. I can't stand the thought of Julie not being with us anymore. Why not take me before taking any of my children? She has never given us an unpleasant hour in her life. The way I feel now, God, all the joys her life has given us pale in comparison to the thought of losing her.*

He drove back to the hotel with his older daughter Kay Lynn. Tomorrow, she would have to return to her work in New York. She sobbed for her sister.
~~~

In the corridor of the hotel, he kissed her good night.

It was after midnight when he went to bed. He started to pray: *Oh God, this has been the longest week.*

~~~

The next day, while Sid and Margaret continued their vigil by Julie's bed, two nurses entered with a wheelchair. "We're getting Julie up now," one of them announced.

The other explained that providing stimulation was normally done with comatose patients. "It helps get them out of a coma," she said.

Sid and Margaret watched. As soon as the nurses started lifting Julie out of her hospital bed, she immediately became agitated. Her eyes remained closed, and she made no sound, but one look at her facial expression made it clear that she was in incredible pain.

The nurses placed her in a sitting position in the wheelchair, ignoring the pain reflected so clearly on her face. They might not have continued placing her in a wheelchair every day thereafter, had they known then that she suffered from a fractured bone in her back. The doctors were reluctant to take more x-rays because she was expecting a baby. Only later did they discover that it was her fractured back that caused her anguish.

Doctors had, however, taken two ultrasound pictures of the tiny embryo. The slight change of position between the two pictures had confirmed that her embryo was alive.

Family members and friends came every day, wanting to see Julie, but that was not allowed. Only parents and siblings could see her in the critical care unit. Those who saw her commented how peaceful and pretty she looked. There was no swelling. No visible injuries. Occasionally she began to open her eyes, but there was no indication that she saw anything or heard her father or the others talking to her. Although unable to make any sounds, she clearly suffered from the daily transition from her bed to a chair. The required sitting position was usually of short duration, but it was painful for Sid to
~~~

watch. She looked much more serene lying in her hospital bed.

Her blood pressure and heart rate remained dangerously high. The doctors were very concerned, giving Sid and Margaret no reason for optimism, though literally thousands of people prayed for her recovery. Entire church congregations as far away as Grand Rapids, Michigan, where many relatives lived, had been asked to pray for healing. Despite the doubts and worries weighing on his shoulders, Sid felt a spark of hope and comfort when he learned of the widespread prayer.

Because Julie was unable to swallow, nutrition was provided via a feeding tube. After two weeks, the nurses began attempting to feed her by mouth. Slowly, she learned to swallow, and soon Margaret was asked to begin feeding her some ice cream. He watched silently from the visitor's chair while Margaret perched on the bed, spooning the ice cream into their daughter's mouth. Memories of years gone by surfaced. He recalled Margaret feeding baby Julie more than twenty years earlier. Now, with the same love and tenderness, she fed her twenty-three-year-old daughter. Later that evening, in their hotel room, Margaret choked back tears as she said, "I wouldn't mind feeding Julie for many years, if only her life would be spared."

Gradually, the fog of the coma lifted. Julie became more alert. Her eyes began to focus on people, and she followed their movements. Sid hoped she was beginning to hear and understand all the loving words relatives and friends spoke to her. She had been moved out of the critical care unit and could now have visitors and make trips beyond her floor.

About three weeks later, he was pushing Julie in a wheelchair along the corridor of the hospital. It was a Sunday, and Margaret had gone with their son Ron's family to church. Like so many years before, Sid was now "babysitting" his grown younger daughter.

He stopped pushing the wheelchair momentarily and

stood in front of Julie. "Shall we go to the cafeteria and get some ice cream, Julie?" he asked.

When she smiled and nodded her approval, joy and gratitude flooded his being.

"Okay," he said. "We'll go to the third floor."

They stopped by the elevator, and amazingly, Julie reached for the button and pushed the *up* arrow. Soon, the door slid open, and he pushed her wheelchair inside. Another surprise: Julie reached out and pushed the button labeled *3*. Not only had she heard him, she had remembered!

In the cafeteria, he positioned her chair by a table, from where she was able to see the location of the ice cream machine. "Okay, Julie, I'm going to get some ice cream for you," he announced.

Again, she smiled. He proceeded to walk in a direction opposite the ice cream machine. Out of the corner of his eye, he could tell her eyes were following. He disappeared around a corner and then peeked back around to see her smiling broadly with an expression that said, *Boy, my dad is stupid.*

When he returned to the table, she looked at him, still wearing that grin and pointing to where the ice cream was. He acted embarrassed and continued to talk about his own stupidity while feeding her ice cream.

What joy they shared with the many visitors who came that Sunday.

Margaret had been to a beauty salon in Everett on Saturday, where the beautician had given her a nice permanent. As she and Sid stood at the foot of Julie's bed that evening, Margaret pointed to her hair and asked, "Do you like my perm, Julie?"

Intently, approvingly, but silently, Julie looked at her mother's beautiful dark hair freshly permed. With a serious expression, Sid looked from Margaret's hair to Julie and said, "That's not a permanent. That's a wig!"

For the first time since her injury, Julie responded with an audible laugh. She knew he was joking.

It was then that her brother Gerald and his wife, Lynne, entered the room. With great excitement, Sid and Margaret told them that Julie had laughed out loud when he belittled her mother's beautiful hair.

He and Ger conspired to invent other funny scenarios. They privately agreed that Sid would pull Ger's chair back just as he was about to sit down. A little later, when Ger hit the floor in an exaggerated display of utter surprise, they all watched as Julie waited a moment to make sure her brother hadn't broken any bones before she laughed and laughed. It was amazing to see how humor had begun to lift the curtain of her coma, as she had just self-administered a dose of life's most powerful medicine: laughter.

~~~

Sid felt incredible relief that they no longer needed to worry about Julie's survival. He knew that months of therapy awaited her. No one knew to what degree the skills of normal living, which everyone takes for granted, Julie would reacquire.

Would she learn to walk again, talk, read, write, feed herself, dress herself, cook, or take care of the baby she was expecting? They didn't know. The doctors didn't, either. They knew her brain injury was serious. When rear-ended by the drunk driver, her head had slammed into the car's headrest. It had then whiplashed into an equally violent forward motion, slamming her head into the steering wheel. This type of injury caused delicate brain tissues to hit against the rough, jagged inner surface of the skull. It was a double whammy in a way similar to taking a raw egg and vigorously shaking it back and forth, scrambling the yoke.

Sid was hopeful and optimistic that with therapy, patience, and time, Julie would be her kind, funny, smart, loving self again. From his observation, he believed that at least to a large degree, her intelligence was intact. He based this on his observation that she quickly assessed things going on around her. Years later, he read about the latest research that sug-
~~~

gested only about six percent of all the gray matter in the brain was related to intelligence.

The first two months of therapy were very difficult for Julie, as well as Sid as he watched her struggle. He was touched by the constant encouragement and help her mother offered every day. It shouldn't have surprised him. Julie was the last of their six children. He knew that her mother's love and dedication to all their children was fathomless.

Intensive therapy sessions started as the grip of the coma lightened. Although, years later, Julie remembered nothing about the first few weeks of her therapy sessions, at the time they were very frustrating for her and painful to watch. She had to learn reading, writing, and arithmetic again, starting at the first-grade level. She often cried because to some degree she knew that she'd learned it all before but didn't know why all that knowledge had disappeared. Why couldn't she walk or talk or read? Why wouldn't her right hand work when she was learning to type again? She knew that she'd been very speedy at the keyboard. How and when had that changed?

Her first memory of that time was of a large white chalkboard hanging on the wall of her hospital room. In large black letters, it read: *My name is Julie Bedient. I am 23 years old. I was hit by a drunk driver. I am married to Mike Bedient. I am expecting a baby*. She was unable to read it aloud, but it registered to the point that she remembered what it said many years later.

The doctors and therapists at the hospital were constantly amazed by the rapid progress their patient was making. Julie, however, always held herself to high standards of performance. Not only did she regard her progress as too slow, but also constantly worried that complete recovery and regaining all her earlier skills entirely might not be realized. This brought many tears of frustration and depression. But her innate sense of humor, with the help of her family, always had a cathartic effect and lifted her spirits.

Over time, the residual deficiencies resulting from her brain injury receded, though some still lingered. Most of the people who crossed her path didn't know about those deficiencies, but they never forgot her friendly smile, pleasant personality, and lively sense of humor.

~~~

Thursday, June 4, 2009, was a very warm day as Sid rode to the Lynden Christian High School graduation program. It was still nearly 90 degrees as he sat next to his wife on the bleachers overlooking the large sports field. His youngest granddaughter was graduating with a perfect 4.0 grade average. He watched with pride as she filed in with eighty fellow graduates. After all the speeches, the diplomas, the special recognitions and awards and scholarships, he left the bleachers. Parents, grandparents, brothers, sisters, and other family members gathered where the graduates would soon appear after the completion of the ceremonies.

He spotted Julie among the crowd, waiting to be the first to congratulate her daughter with a loving embrace and a kiss. Next to her stood a young man of twenty-one, tanned, muscular and strong. Sid thought of the two small x-ray pictures of a tiny embryo, confirming that the embryo had survived the injuries Julie had sustained after that horrible crash so many years ago. Sid had looked at those x-ray pictures many times before he finally watched baby Benjamin enter into the world and take his first crying breath.

Sid felt a lump in his throat as he watched the graduation scene. From deep within his soul, a prayer surfaced. Though not uttered aloud, it was a prayer of enormous gratitude that, instead of losing their beloved daughter, they had been blessed for all those years with the lives of Julie and her two children, Benjamin and Katie.

The motto on the wall of Julie's childhood bedroom came to him again in a moment of spontaneous joy: *Let everything that has breath praise the Lord!*

~~~

From Darkness into Light

I

"Tom, line three is for you. I think it's your wife."

Tom Klarksen thanked his receptionist and picked up the receiver. "Hi, hon, nothing wrong, I hope?"

"Oh no, Tom. You're a worrywart," responded Janelle. "I just thought I'd call and remind you that we have to go to school to hear our daughter sing in her choir."

"Oh, yes. Thanks for reminding me. I'll be home a little early."

Incredible, he thought.

Lonnie was smart and already in the choir at the Christian school in Bellingham that he and Janelle had decided their children would attend. In a few short years, Johnny would begin his grade school education at the same school. How could these enormous changes have happened in his life?

"Okay, love, and I'll have dinner ready a little early tonight," said Janelle. "See you soon."

The telephone connection clicked, but before returning to his work, Tom rested his elbows on the desk, cupped his chin in his hands, and looked out the window. He could understand the teacher wanting her choir students to practice for a little concert. It was a real motivator for the kids when they knew that all their parents would come, as well as brothers and sisters. There would even be uncles and aunts in the audience, and most likely quite a few grandparents as well. That was all the reason Lonnie needed to patiently practice their repertoire of songs.

The ringing telephone of his direct line ended his reverie.

That evening, Tom and Janelle, carrying baby Johnny, walked into the gymnasium of the school. They didn't have to sit in the bleachers; the gymnasium had been converted to an auditorium. They headed for some unoccupied chairs in the first row close to the curtained stage.

Promptly at 7:30 the curtains rose, revealing the choir. Lonnie stood in the first row, smiling nervously. Her long blond hair, neatly styled by Janelle, shone under the stage lights. She spotted her family immediately.

The teacher assumed the place of the director and raised her hands. All choir members fastened their eyes on her. The sweet voices of nearly twenty children filled the auditorium of the small Christian school. Their voices blended and harmonized beautifully as they began to sing:

"There is sunshine in my soul today,
More glorious and bright
Than glows in any earthly sky,
For Jesus is my light.
Oh there's sunshine,
Blessed sunshine,
When the peaceful, happy moments roll;
When Jesus shows his happy face,
There is sunshine in my soul."

There was a brief pause. The director handed a microphone to Lonnie. Then, to the surprise of her parents, the auditorium walls reverberated with her youthful, angelic solo voice. Tom and Janelle glanced at each other with surprise as they listened to their daughter.

"Oh there's sunshine,
Blessed sunshine,
When the peaceful, happy moments roll;
When Jesus shows his happy face,
There is sunshine in my soul."

Tom looked at his wife and clasped his much larger hand over hers. Tears floated in her brown eyes – tears of awe, pride, and gratitude for the moment when, as parents, they heard their daughter expressing the joy of her faith in Jesus publicly on stage in a beautiful voice.

For Tom, this powerful experience was different from any of his own childhood experiences. As the children's choir continued, his mind drifted to an earlier time when he had attended grade school. At that time, he never would have envisioned such a scene as being a part of his future life. He felt moisture filling his own eyes as he realized that had it not been for a heavenly intervention, his life could not have unfolded as it had.

Images and memories of his life in grade school surfaced again.

~~~

As a child, he had never heard of Christianity or a Christian school. Yes, he had learned reading, writing, and arithmetic, but he quickly learned that even in grade school, there were bullies. Usually they were dummies and cowards who wanted to be perceived as bullies. They preyed on kids they perceived as weak. He learned that it was important not to be perceived as weak or "scared." It was equally important not to convey an attitude of cockiness. Early in life, his survival skills were finely honed. He knew the troublemakers and where the threats were lurking. He was often afraid, but he instinctively knew that it was important not to convey the
~~~

appearance of being afraid. He would always do his best to avoid getting into fights.

Tom was a little bigger and heavier than most kids his age, but he never flaunted his physical superiority and avoided all action that would draw attention to him. He knew where the major threats were and often came up with a creative way to connect with a big bully and neutralize him as a threat. He didn't even know the word "psychology."

Knowing that one big bully was on a soccer team, he went to a game and watched him play. The "bully player" didn't know he was there. The following day, during recess, Tom looked him up. The kid watched him approach warily.

Tom put a big smile on his face and said, "Hey, dude, I watched you kick not one but two field goals last night. You're something else. I bet you're gonna make it big in sports, man. I'll be cheerin' for ya."

The kid didn't know how to act or what to say. The boy had probably never heard a word of praise before and stammered a feeble "Thanks," showing a weak smile.

Tom knew that he would never have to worry about that kid or his buddies beating him up. It would be more likely that they would be his protectors, if that were ever needed.

Unlike many students in his class, he always received good grades. His teacher, Miss Knox, frequently praised him in front of the class. It was her way of attempting to motivate the other students, but it made him nervous.

One afternoon when she was next to his desk and looking at him, he looked at her and whispered, "Miss Knox?"

She put her ear close to his mouth.

"Miss Knox," he said, "I really appreciate your praise for my school work, but it makes me nervous."

"Why does it make you nervous, Tommy?" she asked.

"You know, there are kids in class who often get into fights. They like to pick on kids when they're jealous. I don't want to give them a reason to be jealous and pick a fight with me."

Miss Knox stared at him for a moment before whispering, "Tommy, you're even smarter than I thought. I'll comply with your wish."

The strategy worked, and Tom continued to hone his street smarts to survive.

II

Tom parked his car in front of their cozy home and swiftly headed to the front door. It had been a busy day at the office where he worked publishing a local business magazine.

As soon as he opened the door, the fragrance of a delicious dinner, still cooking, assaulted his senses and made him salivate. Quickly he crossed the room to greet his wife and his daughter, who raised her arms in anticipation of the hugs and kisses she was accustomed to getting from her daddy. She would not be disappointed.

He turned to three-year-old Johnny, who sat on the floor in front of the TV set staring at a single, non-moving picture. He had found the "freeze frame" button on the remote.

Quickly pressing the freeze-frame button again, he said, "Look, Daddy, I can do that."

Johnny was a smart, inquisitive little boy. Thanks to his mother's daily tutoring, Johnny could already read simple words. His little brain was like a sponge attempting to absorb the answers his mommy and daddy gave him to all his questions. He seemed to enjoy watching sports on TV even more than playing with his toys.

Johnny looked from the TV screen to his dad. "Daddy, why do boys in red clothes push the boy in green and make him fall? Is it 'cause he's running away with the ball?"

Tom noticed that Johnny was watching cartoon characters playing baseball with a plastic bat. Crouching to the floor and sitting next to his son, he ruffled Johnny's dark hair. "Wow, Johnny, you think you would like to play baseball?"

"Yes, Daddy, can you play with me?"

He hugged his little boy and said, "I'll tell you what we'll do. Right after dinner, you and I are going to go to a store and get us a bat and a ball. I'll pitch the ball to you, and you hit the ball with your bat. Shall we do that?"

He didn't have to wait for an answer. The sheer delight on the boy's face was a more eloquent response than anything he could have said.

A good hour later, Tom pitched a gently curving overhand ball to his little boy. Johnny certainly had watched the cartoon characters closely. There he stood, a determined look on his face. Holding the plastic bat high in the air, he waited for the baseball to arrive. *POW!* Tom ducked as the ball just barely missed his head.

After ten pitches and ten hits, it was Johnny's bedtime. Tom looked at his little boy with amazement. Johnny had remarkable hand-eye coordination at such an early age. Tom was a very proud father as he tucked his son into bed that evening. After sharing Johnny's earliest athletic accomplishments with his wife, he settled into his easy chair with the day's newspaper.

Tom picked up the daily newspaper and curled up on the couch. Instead of concentrating on reading, he couldn't help but look at his wife as she ushered Lonnie to bed. He admired her immensely. Not only because he had married a beautiful young lady, but also because she was the most loving and caring young mother he could ever imagine. For long moments, he stared into space. He knew beyond the shadow of a doubt, with a deep sense of gratitude, that his children would never have to experience the tragedies, fears and dangers that had marked the first eighteen years of his own life. He also knew that his own dad had never relished the serene beauty of the family life he now enjoyed.

Tom thought about his three-year-old son. His mind drifted to his own childhood, a thousand miles away, when he was three years old. Normally, at the age of three, memories are rarely retained. His memories, however, were painfully crystal-clear. He recalled the last time he had seen his biological father, but he banned the thought from his mind. He knew the memories of nightmarish events of his youth would likely continue to invade his consciousness many times throughout his life.

Despite his best efforts, the fears of his youth crept into his consciousness. How different his life would have been in California. Images of crime, hatred, evil, gangs, and violence played vividly in his mind.

~~~

His family lived in Oxnard, California. From overhearing adult conversation, he had learned that Oxnard had the third-highest crime rate of cities in California. His family home was right in the middle of a crime-ridden neighborhood. Even at a young age, he knew he wanted something different – different from everything he saw around him.

Children usually learn life development skills from their parents or older siblings. From parents they can normally be expected to learn guidance, direction, and protection. Of course, he didn't understand that as a child, nor did he understand at that time that his family was completely dysfunctional. He assumed that all the experiences he observed as a child were normal.

At the age of five, while he waited in line at the grocery store with his mother, a kid from his kindergarten class and his entire family stood in the check stand behind them. They looked like such a nice family.

"Where's your dad?" the kid asked him curiously.

Tom changed the subject and started joking around to distract him from the question and from seeing his mom pay for their groceries with food stamps.

He was eleven years old and in sixth grade when he first gained an understanding of drugs. It was the year he first smoked marijuana. His older brother Chris was in eighth grade and associated with people who experimented with drugs. In junior high school, if you had money, you could get
~~~

pot as easily as buying candy. One night, he went with his brother to his friend Larry's house a few doors down from where they lived. Although he knew many other people who had used drugs, this was where he was first introduced to pot. It seemed harmless, very similar to when he had tried a cigarette for the first time in the first grade.

Larry had a water bong, which was the most efficient way to smoke. It was a glass or plastic pipe that you filled with water. You sucked the burning pot through a stem while the smoke came up through the bong. You got 100 per cent of the smoke. Larry showed him how to use it. At the time, it was a fun and exciting experience. While Tom continued to smoke now and then, two things stopped him from doing it regularly: the cost, and the fact that he was a very competitive athlete and realized that he could not be competitive if he smoked.

His brother Chris didn't have that motivation. One day, a couple of gang members came up to him in an effort to intimidate him. He literally decked one of them and threatened the second one, who immediately backed down. Tom was always more scared for his brother than he was for himself.

Another time, Tom was walking home from school with his brother. A car pulled up in front of them, and immediately he knew they were going to be in a situation. Three guys got out. Tom pleaded with Chris to get the heck out of there, but just like when he was drunk, he would have nothing to do with little brother's advice. Two of the guys approached Chris with confidence and pointed him out to the third, who pulled out a switchblade knife. The big kid said he was there to teach Chris a lesson, while the other two confirmed it with cockiness. Tom was terrified for his brother. His mind went blank. He had no idea how to get out of this confrontation.

As it turned out, he didn't need to. His brother charged the guy. Before he could even swing the knife, Chris had the guy on the ground and was pounding him in the face. His nose and mouth were bloody, but Chris didn't stop. Tom told him to quit, but it was like he couldn't stop. It was the first time he realized that his brother had something in him that was not at all rational. That scared him more than any threats he had faced previously.

Chris finally got off the guy he was beating. He turned to the other two, whose confidence and cockiness had completely evaporated. Clearly, they were no longer a threat. As Tom walked away with his brother, the two victims attended to the one who was still on the ground.

Chris's stock at school rose as the story spread the following day. He did not seem to realize that he had just become a bigger target for retaliation.

III

Sitting at the dinner table, Tom looked at his son, now thirteen years old. "Johnny, you'd better eat your dinner. You've got a big game tonight."

Johnny looked down at his plate with a slight frown. "I'm not hungry."

Tom knew he must be a little nervous about the championship basketball game that night. It would be held in a big high school gymnasium, and there would be many spectators. Johnny's team would be playing against a big team and the only one in the youth league with a name: the Golden Nickels. All five of their starters believed they were the Golden Five. Most of them were taller than the guys on his son's team. The two teams had already played once this season, and that was the only game Johnny's team had lost by a big margin. The Golden Nickels hadn't lost a game all season.

"Your nervousness is understandable," Tom said. "They're a proud bunch. They may already think that they have it in the bag. After all, they probably think, 'It's just the team from that little Christian school.' They may think it's going to be a slam dunk. But that's dangerous thinking, Johnny, and your team may have a surprise for them."

Johnny looked unimpressed. "I'm still nervous."

Tom looked into his son's kind brown eyes, and for a moment he reflected on how much he always loved looking into the kind brown eyes of his wife. Yes, Johnny had his mother's eyes.

"Don't worry about being nervous," he reassured his son. "Everybody gets nervous before a big performance. Daddy gets nervous every time before he has to give a speech to a large audience. On the basketball court, you'll turn your nervousness into energy. That speedy little guard from the Christian school will give those 'Golden Five' their nickel's worth."

Finally, Johnny looked at his dad with a smile. "Thanks, Dad."

It was at least forty-five minutes before the start of the ballgame when they arrived at the large high school where the Youth League championship game was scheduled. None of the players were yet of driving age, which accounted for the fact that nearly all the parents of the players were already at the school. As a few early spectators arrived, it was easy for the Klarksen family to find good seating. Tom chose a seat in the fourth row of the bleachers. This would allow him a good view of all the action on the court. Lonnie and his wife, Janelle, followed him. They all had to deal with some nervous 'butterflies in the stomach' in anticipation of watching the game.

It wasn't long before the young players of both teams appeared on the court. They all wore their warm-up sweaters as they began their series of practice routines. Basketballs sailed for the basket from all directions as each player practiced his long shots. As the Klarksen family watched, Johnny rarely missed a shot.

As Tom looked at the opposing team, he noticed that they were generally a little taller than Johnny's team. *Kids learn more from losing a game than they do from winning*, he thought. He didn't know whether he wanted to use that thought to comfort Johnny after losing the game, or if it was a wishful thought applicable to the cocky "Golden Five." Suddenly, there was an ear-piercing buzzer sound, and both teams rushed into their locker rooms.

A few minutes later, the other team members were introduced by the announcer holding a microphone. Tom and Janelle couldn't avoid looking at each other with pride as their son's name boomed from the speakers. "Shooting guard Johnny Klarksen," the announcer proclaimed.

Tom had an intimate knowledge of the game. He had once been a "stand-out" player and had worked as a coach and a referee. He knew that point guard was one of the most difficult of the five positions to play on the floor. The point guard was responsible for getting his team into its offense, making sure all of the players were aware of their roles on the floor, and, above all, creating scoring opportunities for both the players around him and himself – in that order. One of the most difficult responsibilities of playing point guard was the need to have his mind moving in several directions at once. He had to recognize and respond to the type of defense that the opposition was playing, and make sure his players were in the correct spots. Also, he was the only player within the offensive structure that had to juggle his responsibilities, both as defender, passer, and scorer.

Now, with his officiating duties in the past, Tom was simply glued to his seat as he watched every move Johnny made. Of course, he and Janelle had never missed attending one of Johnny's games. But as they glanced at each other again, they both knew this was the biggest game of young Johnny's life.

The tempo of the game was fast and furious. Offensively, the little team from the little Christian school made basket after basket. Johnny was faster than most of his defenders. He rarely missed a shot. When he was "double-teamed," he would quickly spot a teammate in the open and would pass the ball.

Early in the second quarter, the Golden Nickels called a time-out. They huddled around their coach, some of them pointing and glancing at Johnny. Their team was down by nineteen points. They'd never been down by more than one or two points in any of their games. They hadn't lost a game for two seasons. What was happening?

Their coach was talking to his center. He was the biggest boy on the team. But this "Johnny" of the other team was giving him fits defensively. This little kid was quick and stuck to him like glue. Tom guessed that it was preventing him from running his team's offense as he was used to. Likely, he had never experienced it before, and this championship game was putting a real crimp in his ego.

Both teams returned to the floor, and the game resumed. Johnny's fierce defense of the opposing point guard often resulted in the big kid being whistled for a double-dribble call. That always resulted in a turnover. It was nearly halftime when it happened.

The big point guard had passed the ball to a teammate as he was heading for the backcourt for an easy lay-up. He expected his teammate to pass him the ball again as soon as he was in good backcourt position. Johnny stayed on him tight without fouling him, waving his hand in front of the kid's eyes. Johnny wasn't nearly as tall. The big point guard quickly looked for the two referees. Realizing that, just for a moment, he was in the referee's blind spot, he punched his elbow violently into Johnny's left eye.

Johnny let out a painful scream and fell backward to the floor. His fall was partially buffered by a nearby teammate.

While most of the spectators saw that Johnny had just received an intentional, flagrant foul, the refs had not seen it. There was no whistle. Johnny's coach signaled time-out and rushed to the injured boy's aid, along with others.

Tom and Janelle watched in horror. Reflexively, Tom jumped to his feet and yelled, "Hey refs, are you guys blind?"

All the while yelling, he raced for the stairway.

Fortunately, someone else jumped up and stood in Tom's way. It was his friend Karl.

"Get out of my way, Karl," Tom yelled. He was in a fit of uncontrollable anger. Some kid had hurt his Johnny. He wanted to check on his son, and he wanted to jerk a big tuft of pitch-black hair out of the big kid's head.

Karl put his arms around Tom's midriff and held his ground. "I saw what happened, Tom. The refs didn't see it, but nearly all of the people here did, including the coaches on both sides. I think Johnny is going to be okay, and I'm sure the big kid hasn't seen the end of this. You can only make things worse, Tom. Calm down, sit by Janelle, hold her hand, and wait for Johnny to come out of the locker room."

Even though his eyes were still blazing, Tom said, "I know you're right." Without another word, he wiped perspiration from his forehead and sat close to Janelle, clasping her hand in his. She was crying. She was worried. Tom needed to comfort and reassure both Janelle and his daughter Lonnie.

During the entire third quarter, the coach of the Golden Nickels team kept his point guard on the bench. Early in the fourth quarter, their team was still down by eleven points when the coach allowed his point guard back into the game. Within a short time, the Golden Nickels had closed their deficit score to within five points. That's when Johnny was escorted from the locker room. He sat down next to his coach, who looked at the bulging bandage on Johnny's left eye. The bulging was undoubtedly due to an ice pack, which would prevent excessive swelling of the injury.

Johnny saw the score. He kept talking to the coach and pointing to the scoreboard. Knowing his son, Tom knew that he was pleading with the coach to allow him back into the game. He knew that the coach would worry about his shooting ability with one eye covered. He wouldn't be able to see the floor action in three dimensions. It would likely hamper his distance perception, as well as his shooting and passing accuracy. He whispered to Johnny and called time-out.

After the time-out, Johnny raced back onto the court. Time was running out, and the team was up by only two points. Immediately, Johnny signaled to pass him the inbound ball. He caught it with lightning speed, dribbled left, then right, then left again, before glancing at the hoop and making a giant leap in the air while shooting the ball. *Swish*, it passed right through the middle of the hoop. In a flash, he was back on the big center again and forced another turnover.

The buzzer heralded the end of the championship game. Johnny's team had won by three points.

The basketball floor broke out in wild pandemonium. Soon order was restored, and it was trophy time. Johnny was handed the trophy. He raised it high above his head and reveled in the shouting and clapping of the excited fans. Then both teams lined up in single file. It was tradition to file past each other while each player gave a high-five to the players of the opposite team. When Johnny came to his black-haired nemesis, he raised his hand. The boy looked the other way and refused to reciprocate. Johnny simply smiled. The game was over.

~~~

Tom drove to the side door of the building where the team would exit to be picked up by their parents. It was a cold, clear winter day, and he left the engine running and the heater on warm. That would keep his wife and daughter comfortable in the backseat while he waited for Johnny. While he stood just outside the door, it was clear from the excited voices coming from the locker room that the team was still celebrating their unexpected victory.

Finally, Johnny emerged dressed and flanked by his coach. He searched the waiting parents. "There's my dad," said Johnny as he pointed in Tom's direction.

The coach headed straight for Tom. "Congratulations, Mr. Klarksen," he said as he grasped Tom's hand and shook it vigorously. "Johnny played an amazing game. We're worried
~~~

about the injury to his eye, and we're angry about the deliberate way the injury was inflicted. It may not be a bad idea to stop at the emergency room and have a doctor check on the eye. We're very sorry about that."

Tom put his arm around Johnny's shoulders, and they walked to the family car.

As soon as his mom and sister saw them, they rushed out of the car to give Johnny a big hug and congratulations. "How's your eye?" asked Janelle while looking at the large bandage covering his eye and the surrounding area.

"It hurts a little, but it'll be okay," said Johnny. "I think the big kid from the other team didn't mean to hurt me."

For a moment, Tom thought about what he had just heard. Then he looked at his wife and said, "The coach recommended we stop at the emergency room and have the injury checked by a doctor."

"That's a good idea, hon," she replied with concern. "Let's do that."

Both Tom and Janelle stayed with Johnny as the doctor examined him. As soon as the thick patch was removed, they could all see Johnny's bloody eye now nearly swollen closed, surrounded by a huge blue bruise. To prevent infection, the doctor explained that Johnny would be given a shot. He would have to keep a small blue bag with ice over his injured eye at all times, to be replaced about every hour. He should return for a follow-up visit the next day.

~~~

Tom urged his wife to go to bed. He wanted to stay in Johnny's room and replace the ice pack every hour. He needed time to think – to think about his son wanting to believe that the bully from the other basketball team hadn't meant to hurt him. Johnny was such a kind, loving, gentle boy. Tom and Janelle raised their children in a devout Christian home. Early in their lives their children had learned to sing "Jesus Loves Me." Mommy and Daddy loved them. They always felt loved and secure. They had not yet expe-
~~~

rienced evil in their youthful world.

The sudden buzzing sound emanating from the radio was the sound of the alarm which he had set to remind him that every hour he needed to put a fresh cold ice pack on Johnny's swollen eye. He quickly retrieved a fresh pack from the freezer compartment. Johnny was sleeping. Oh, how he hated to awaken him.

He carefully removed the old ice pack and placed a small handkerchief over the swollen eye. Tenderly he placed the ice pack on top of the handkerchief. Johnny didn't even stir.

Tom sat in his chair again. He could easily sleep for an hour, but slumber seemed far away. He thought of the reminiscing he had done about his own childhood. He knew that his experiences were in no way analogous to what Johnny had experienced earlier in the evening. He had never known love. He had been exposed to evil nearly every day. He had often done the wrong thing. How could he prepare his children for the reality that, sooner or later, they would encounter evil? How could they make choices? Wasn't it the parents' responsibility to teach their children to make the right choices? His body shuddered involuntarily. He could have easily become a criminal.

The buzzing of the alarm made him jump. He headed for the couch where Johnny was sleeping.

But Johnny wasn't sleeping. He was wide-awake as his dad asked him, "How are you feeling?"

"My head hurts. I can't sleep."

"The doctor told us to give you a Tylenol if you get a headache. I'll get one for you to swallow with some water. And I'll get a fresh ice pack for your swollen eye."

Tom tenderly lifted his son's head as he gave him the pill with some water. He planted a kiss on Johnny's forehead. "Okay, try to go back to sleep. The Tylenol will soon make much of your headache go away."

Johnny looked his dad in the eyes and said, "The big

kid that hit me in the eye with his elbow, you don't think he did that accidentally, Dad?"

Tom pulled up a chair next to the couch. "No, Johnny, that was not an accident. It was a flagrant foul intended to hurt you. The refs didn't see it, but I did. And most of the people in the gym saw it."

Johnny closed his eyes. "That would be mean, wouldn't it?"

"Yes, some people can be very mean."

Johnny put his hand to his forehead and looked at the ceiling. Then he turned to his dad again and said, "That boy must not be a Christian."

"I don't know. Even some people who consider themselves Christians can do some very mean things."

"I would never want to be mean and purposely hurt other people."

"I know you wouldn't, son, but there is a lot of evil in this world. When I was your age, I saw more evil in a few years of my youth than I hope and pray you'll see in your entire life."

Johnny tried to sit up. He seemed to be struggling with this new information. Tom knew he must have questions he wanted to ask.

"Dad, did you ever do mean things to other people?"

Tom had not expected that question. Father and son looked at each other without speaking.

Finally, Tom broke the silence. "I grew up amidst evil. I could do any good or bad thing I wanted to do. I was not a Christian. But Johnny, your head is sore, and you need to sleep now and get better. We'll talk about it later."

"Can I ask you one more question?"

"Sure."

"How did you become a Christian?"

Tom patted his son's head. "Johnny, you need sleep now. Sometime soon, I'll tell you and your sister the whole story about the first eighteen years of my life. Then I'll answer your question. Then I'll tell you about a miracle."

"A real miracle?" asked Johnny.

"Yes, Johnny, nothing less than a miracle. Good night, son."

IV

Icy water droplets pelted against his office window. It was early afternoon, and Tom sat at his desk. Concentrating on his work, he was unaware of the ice storm that had started raging nearly an hour earlier. He looked outside through his office window. A thin film of ice forming on the window distorted the view.

"All Bellingham schools were closed nearly an hour ago," he overheard one of his staff saying to another.

"Yes, all schoolkids were bussed home," another responded.

Tom jumped up as if he had just become acquainted with the healthy shock of a cattle prod. He knew his wife would have received a call from the Christian school to pick up their two children. He grabbed his coat and yelled to his staff, "See you later," as he rushed out the door.

A moment later, he lay flat on his back on the sidewalk. Slowly and painfully, he checked to see if his legs would still support his body. He realized that after growing up in Southern California, his experience with ice was still limited.

Much more carefully now, he made his way to his car and started it. The windshield was covered with a sheet of ice. Since he didn't have an ice scraper in the car, he decided to just wait until the heater temperature increased enough to defrost his windshield and rear window. Waiting and shivering, he dialed his home number to talk to his wife.

"Hi, hon, do you have the kids home already?" he asked.

"Yes, I got them home just before it got really slippery. Are you on your way?"

"I will be as soon as the car heats up enough to defrost the windshield. I learned the hard way about the slippery ice."

"What do you mean?"

"Coming out of my office to race to the car, I promptly fell on my butt."

"I'm glad you've got a little padding there," Janelle kidded. "I've been watching some cars trying to make it up the hill to our neighborhood. They're slipping and sliding. I noticed a service truck coming to put chains on the rear wheels. You should have them put on before trying to make it up the hill."

"Oh, it shouldn't be that bad. I'll check it out. See you in about fifteen minutes. I love you."

"I love you, too."

After he had to return to the office and ask some of his people to help get his slightly forward-sloping car out of its parking area, he decided that it would be best to have a service station install chains on all four wheels of his car. It was nearly seven o'clock that evening when he walked through the door of his home.

~~~

The next morning, he quietly walked to his children's bedrooms. Both were still sound asleep. They knew that there would be no school today. Even his normally early bird wife was still sleeping. He walked into their large living room with the big picture window overlooking the big lake. What he saw was the most amazing winter wonderland he could imagine. The freezing rain had turned to large snowflakes, which now covered the landscape with a blanket of white purity. The branches of the evergreen trees bowed under the heavy load. Smoke from the neighbor's fireplace chimney curled straight up, completely undisturbed in the cold, quiet air. The freshly fallen snow glinted like silver-speckled satin. Had he stayed in Southern California, he never would have seen the beauty of such an idyllic winter morning.

Suddenly, still staring out the window, his thoughts
~~~

turned to that place where he had spent the first eighteen years of his life. There was so much about those eighteen years in California that he didn't want to tell his children. When he was tending Johnny's injured eye, he had promised his son that he would answer his questions. There was no school today, and his children were home. Even though the thought made him nervous, this was probably a good opportunity for them to learn that not all children grew up in a home with loving, God-fearing parents. He had worried at times that they assumed most children everywhere grew up in a nurturing, sheltered environment. How could they truly appreciate and be grateful for the blessings of their youth if they didn't know how different it was for most children on the planet – how different it had been for their own father? Yes, it was his parental responsibility, no matter how heavy it weighed on him or how difficult it might be.

~~~

The children were very excited during family breakfast time. They couldn't wait to bundle up and play in the snow.

"Kids, you can enjoy this awesome winter weather all morning, but be careful," Tom warned. "It's very slippery, because under that layer of snow is a sheet of pure ice."

"Can we see the ice, Daddy?" asked Lonnie.

"No, honey, that's exactly what makes it dangerous. If you're not super careful, you'll fall flat on your face in a flash. I learned that yesterday already when I fell on my rear. It still hurts."

"We'll be careful," the kids responded almost in unison, and began dashing for extra clothing in the closet when they heard him stop them.

When he had their attention, he said, "Right after lunch, we're going to have a family conference in the living room. It's very important. Now have fun, and don't break any bones."

An hour later, they were all seated around the living room table. Brother and sister looked at their parents and con-
~~~

cluded that their faces looked serious.

"When I was tending to Johnny's injured eye a few weeks ago," Tom began, "he asked me a question, and I promised him that I would answer it. Today I want to do that, and more."

Johnny looked at him with a solemn expression of curiosity. "What do you mean 'and more,' Daddy?" he asked.

"Mom and I believe you are old enough, and I want to tell you about my youth."

"Is there a lot about your youth that Mom doesn't know yet?" asked Lonnie, looking uneasily from one parent to another.

"No, Lonnie, before I married your mom, I told her everything about my life before I was a Christian. Yes, it was risky. I loved that beautiful young lady then no less than I do today. She could have rejected me. But she knew I was honest with her. We both knew that if a marriage was to succeed, there would be no room for dishonesty or deception ever. It will invariably destroy a marriage. We both wanted a family, and I wanted my wife to be the best mother our children could possibly have." Tom paused and looked at his children. While a slight smile played across his face, he asked, "Did I succeed?"

Both children gave a powerful, unexpected answer. They jumped from their seats and kissed their parents with a loud, "I love you, Mom! I love you, Dad!"

Tom and Janelle hugged their children and proclaimed their love for them.

As the children returned to their seats, Tom stared out of the large plate glass window. He didn't see the winter scenery. Tears welled in his eyes. He didn't try to hide them. It was very quiet.

He looked at his wife, then at his son and daughter, as he began, "Children, I am going to share with you my childhood experiences. Some of it is very painful, and all of it is so different from yours. You just showed us love that I had never seen at your age. Until your mother came into my life, no one had ever said to me, 'Tom, I love you.'"

"But Dad," Johnny piped up, "you always knew that Jesus loves you, didn't you?"

Tom shook his head. "The first eighteen years of my life, I didn't have anyone who loved me. I didn't know Jesus loved me. I didn't know God and had no connection with Him. I lived my life strictly by my own conscience. Nobody ever told me what was right or wrong, good or bad. Later, I often wondered where my conscience had come from. Was there something in me that helped me determine what was right and what was wrong? I still ponder that."

The children stared at him wide-eyed. Tom could tell that they were loaded with questions.

Lonnie spoke first. "Daddy, you mean your mom and dad never told you 'I love you' when you were little?"

He nodded sadly. "That's right. Our family was dysfunctional. We were on government welfare and food stamps. My father was a serial criminal, drug addict, and alcoholic, and regularly abused his wife and children both physically and mentally.

"He terrorized my older brother and sister with threats of horrific violence. He once pinned my older brother on the basement floor and drove a butcher knife into the floor next to his head for what he considered whining. The last time I saw my father was one evening when he'd been drinking. He was upset at something, so my mother ordered all the kids to go to their bedrooms. My brother, sister, and I listened as our dad yelled at our mother and beat her up. Later, he took his anger out on the cuckoo clock. On the hour, when it began to ring, he pulled out one of his many guns and shot at it. He left before the police arrived.

"Later that night, Mother took us to our grandparents' house. Several police cars arrived later. My father had called my grandparents, saying he was coming over to kill us and everyone else in the house. That evening was the last time I saw him." Tom swallowed and stared out over the snow-covered lake, adding in almost a whisper, "I was only three years old."

Lonnie, not normally at a loss for words, turned in her chair and also stared out of the large window at the peaceful winter scene outside. Both children were clearly struggling to form a mental image of the unthinkable experiences of their father's childhood. They remained silent until Tom spoke again.

"Even though I don't think that there are kids in your school who are into drugs, I'm sure that you've heard about kids using all kinds of dangerous habit-forming substances. When I was a kid, I could have found drugs anytime I wanted. Marijuana was simple to find. I could walk out my front door, and in minutes, be at any one of four or five locations where I could get it. It would be just as easy to get it at school if I wanted. Cocaine, speed, angel dust, and other drugs were accessible, but more difficult to get, primarily because criminal penalties made the risk of dealing them higher, so the dealers were more discerning about who they would allow in their homes. Because of my brother's friends, I would be welcome to buy what I wanted if I had the money.

"Most of the drug dealers at the street level in our neighborhood were very popular. Most were high school students or recent graduates. They had money. They had nice cars, motorcycles, and other toys, and always had the best parties with the most girls there. Drugs were used at all the parties."

"Were you a drug addict when you were a kid?" Lonnie asked timidly, as if afraid to hear the answer.

Tom shook his head. "No, and I'll tell you why. I took great pride in my athletic ability. I knew that if I got into drugs, my athletic proficiency would deteriorate. I knew the drug addicts. As students and as athletes, they were losers and would never succeed at anything as long as they were addicted to drugs or alcohol. I knew their popularity would be short-term.

"A good friend of my next-door neighbor lived directly across the street from my high school. He dealt drugs from his home. People would be coming and going from that house all day long. There were always several cars in the driveway. Everyone in school knew what was going on there. He was later convicted of trafficking in narcotics and sent to prison."

"Daddy, didn't your mom teach you that using drugs was wrong?" asked Johnny.

Deep in thought, Tom remained silent. From where he was sitting, he could just see the plaque hanging on the wall in the front entry foyer: *Home, where your story begins*. He thought about Oxnard, California, where his story had begun. But this was here and now.

Slowly he shook his head. "No, Johnny, she never did. It seems like everything I learned, I learned on my own by observing. There were never any talks about what to do or not do. No talks about sex, education, politics, religion, or anything important. I simply learned through observation. I began to notice how people behaved, what I liked in people and what I didn't. I began to model people. However, when I was young, there was no accountability, which gave me much more opportunity to make big mistakes with no consequences. The only thing stopping me from doing what was wrong, but fun, was my own conscience. I didn't always listen to it, but it was clearly there. I knew what was right and what was wrong. I could tell the difference between good and bad. I still often ponder where that came from. I didn't know anything about God or Jesus or the Holy Spirit. I know now that even then, They knew me."

It was quiet again. Tom could tell that his children were trying to absorb what he had just told them. Perhaps he could help them a little.

"Kids, I know it's hard to understand how I could possibly know anything about the difference between good and evil in the absence of knowing anything about God's commandments. It was a few years later that I would begin to understand. But first I need to tell you a little about my high school years."

"Did you get into fights?" Johnny piped up enthusiastically.

Seeing his son's interest, Tom smiled ruefully. "My start in high school was a preview of what I needed to get used to. The summer prior to my freshman year, I had just come out of the gymnasium on campus after selecting my freshman classes. I was looking down at my registration form and not really paying attention to what was going on around me. As I looked up, my antenna immediately rose. Three gang members were walking in my direction."

"Did you have gangs in your school?" Lonnie asked, wide-eyed.

Tom nodded. "There were gangs everywhere. They were usually divided by race, mostly black and Mexican. That day, when I came out of the gym after enrolling for my freshman classes, two gang members approached me. I knew them from my early childhood. They were walking directly toward me from across campus in a menacing fashion. It seemed odd to me, because both of them were kids I sort of knew, and I felt confident that I wouldn't be threatened by them under normal circumstances. As they got closer, though, they pulled out switchblades.

"I began to back-pedal and turned to run, when behind me I saw a kid who looked even more scared than I was. His eyes were like golf balls, and he took off running. Both gang members proceeded to chase him. My sense of relief that they were not after me was tempered by the thought that the campus was surrounded by a barbed-wire fence, and that this kid was going to have a difficult time getting away without getting hurt. I didn't want to see anyone being stabbed. I got away that time, but I didn't always get away from danger no matter how I tried to avoid it at all costs. Sometimes it's unavoidable."

"Tell us, Daddy," asked Johnny.

"Okay, I'll tell you one event to give you an idea what life was like for me when I was about your age."

~~~

Tom recalled how he had been on his way home from school one afternoon when he saw a group of at least four kids approaching. He pretended not to look. Draining channels on each side of the road prevented an unobtrusive getaway. He saw the leader of the gang pointing at him. The kid was big and looked strong. There was no escape route other than a foot race, and Tom knew he would probably lose that race.

It was time for an emergency plan. He'd never had to use it before.

He resolutely kept walking, but the distance between him and the gang members was getting short. As his eyes locked in on the bully, Tom reminded himself not to show fear.

A confrontation was unavoidable. He was scared to death but didn't show it. Instead, he put a self-confident smile on his face and pretended to just keep walking along. He knew they weren't going to let him go by without a challenge.

"Hey, pretty boy, you sissy, you think you's cute, don't ya? Hey, white boy, have you ever had your ugly face rearranged a bit?"

Tom was scared to death, but they didn't know that, and he knew he couldn't show his fright. He looked squarely at the leader without showing a trace of fear and said, "Almost. They just miscalculated a little. They underestimated me. I think you bullies will make exactly the same mistake. You look stupid enough." With eyes blazing, he continued with increasing volume, "As soon as the first one of you lays a hand on me, your leader will get the same treatment as another bully who thought he was the toughest dude out West. In all his life, that creep will never forget what happened next." While putting his right hand menacingly in his
~~~

pocket, he yelled, "Just like the bully before you, he couldn't even duck before I'd cut his ear plumb off with my switch-blade. All in a flash, even before the kid could start screaming, with his eyes bulging, I'd stomped his ear in the dirt so it could never be reattached. You may even have seen him. He runs when he sees me. Now move over, and I'll be on my way."

With their mouths hanging open, they watched as he pushed himself between them and continue on his way. He had out-intimidated them, even without any kind of switch-blade in his pocket. It boosted his self-confidence. He felt heroic even as he trembled with fear.

~~~

"Don't misunderstand," Tom said to his children, who listened with rapt attention. "I was a normal, fun-loving kid. I never cut anybody's ear off. I didn't want to lose one of my ears, either. The violent backdrop was simply how life was. I didn't know anything different, and I wasn't particularly scared. I had virtually no parental restraints. I knew how the system worked. To a certain degree, I viewed it as a game. At times I purposefully placed myself in dangerous situations just for the challenge, fun, and thrill of it. How and why, I didn't know then, but what I did know, beyond the shadow of a doubt, was that most of the gang members, bullies, and troublemakers would become lifelong criminals, and I knew at an early age that I didn't want any part of that."

The children looked at each other. They looked at their mother. The kind of life their father described was simply unfathomable to them.

Tom could tell that a question was burning on the tip of Lonnie's tongue. He looked at her with an expression that invited her question.

"Dad?" she began, and then stopped as if she were afraid to ask.

"Go ahead," he prompted. "You may ask me any question you want."
~~~

Nervously, she asked, "Dad, did . . . did Mom know all of this before you were married?"

Tom gazed at his wife. He didn't have to think about the answer. He stood and walked around the table to where Janelle was sitting. Planting a kiss on her forehead, he said, "Lonnie, I'm so glad you asked that question. You know why?" Lonnie fidgeted with the sleeve of her warm winter sweater. Tom didn't wait for a response. "You're a young teenager now. Your question tells me that you're already thinking about things that may well become enormously important for the rest of your life. You already know that I was not a Christian growing up in California. But when I met your mother, I was a Christian. I had matured significantly in my belief in the power and grace of God before we met. I was deeply in love with my beautiful girlfriend."

He smiled at Janelle while the children repeatedly repositioned themselves in their chairs. They were undoubtedly a little nervous because the conversation was getting close to romance.

Tom continued, "I knew that before our relationship could grow and flourish, I'd have to tell her everything about myself. I sought first and foremost someone who would accept me and who would share my life values and my enthusiasm about growing spiritually. We would also have to agree about the kind of family we would like. I wanted her to have no higher priority than being an outstanding mother to my children." Somewhat mischievously, he looked at his wife and added, "I also wanted someone who could pitch and catch a baseball, someone who was a college graduate, and preferably someone who had a background that would allow her to understand mine. I found all of that and more in your mother. Do you kids agree?"

Both Lonnie and Johnny clapped their hands enthusiastically.

It was time for a break. Janelle heated some apple cider and served her family the spicy winter drink with a cookie.

Johnny nuzzled up to his dad and said, “Do you have more scary stories about your life in California?”

Tom smiled. “Okay, Johnny. I’ll tell you one more.” He considered which story to tell. He wanted his son to know that the world could be a tough place, that there would be times when he simply couldn’t just turn the other cheek.

“Don’t forget to tell us about the miracle,” Johnny chided.

“I won’t. I’ll save that for last.”

Lonnie took the dishes to the kitchen, looked out at the beautiful winter landscape outside, and took her place at the table again.

“It was July fourth, after my senior year of high school,” Tom began. “I was ten days away from my eighteenth birthday . . .”

~~~

Tom and a friend of his, Jeff, had been looking for a good party to attend that evening. They were aware of a few different parties that were going on, but didn’t directly know the hosts of any of them. They had been invited to these parties secondhand. It was always a good idea to be aware of who was throwing the party and who was going to be there. There had been an increasing number of shootings over the previous couple of years, many of them taking place at parties, and they wanted to make sure they didn’t wander into enemy territory.

The party they chose was located in Ventura, near the beach. Tom always felt more comfortable near the beach. That was usually the safest place to be if you were white. Tom and Jeff drove by the party first, and it seemed to be in full swing. There were lots of people in the front yard and driveway, as well as in the house. While it appeared to be mixed-race, there were enough white people evident that Tom and Jeff decided to find a place to park.

They hadn’t been in the driveway for more than five minutes when Jeff ran into someone he knew whom Tom did
~~~

not. They were all standing in a small circle. Tom was scanning around the front yard and driveway to see if he recognized anyone he knew when he noticed a guy whose eyes were locked on him. He immediately recognized the look as aggressive. This guy was a threat. His look was intimidating. He wore gang colors, which Tom identified by the color of the bandana hanging from his pocket. He looked plain mean. Tom was a pretty good-sized kid, with a 6'3" frame holding 200 pounds. This guy probably weighed forty pounds more. He was fat, but big, and was standing with about five other guys, all Mexican. He was definitely the bad apple of the group.

Tom had seen that aggressive look before and knew exactly what to do: look away and pretend to ignore it, which he did. About a minute later, he glanced over quickly to confirm that his strategy had worked. It had not. The guy's eyes were still locked on Tom. He had a scowl on his face, and his head bobbed up and down. Tom quickly looked away again, pretending he hadn't noticed him.

It was time to employ strategy B. Tom needed to get out of his line of sight. There was something about him that the guy didn't like. Tom was white, with blond hair, and his size probably represented a good opportunity for the guy to prove his significance to his friends. Tom turned to Jeff and was waiting patiently for the best opportunity to interrupt his conversation and suggest that they move along, when out of nowhere, the lights went off. All he saw was a flash, and he was on the ground. The gang member had cold-cocked him.

Tom may have seen it coming had the attacker not come from his left side. He had been legally blind in his left eye since he was young.

The attacker had hit Tom in the mouth. His lip swelled up immediately, and blood dripped from it. It didn't really hurt. Tom was more shocked than anything else. He quickly regained his equilibrium and stood up.

The guy stood in front of Tom, with his friends behind

him. "You have enough, white boy, or you want some more?'"

Tom wanted to hit him, but he couldn't. He was scared. He presented a pretty good target, but all he felt was fear. His friend Jeff was saying, "Kick his butt, Tom."

Tom didn't have a moral problem with fighting. He was paralyzed by fear. He told Jeff, "Let's get out of here," and started walking away.

"Get the hell out of here, white boy," the attacker called after him.

On the walk up the street, Jeff was saying, "You should have retaliated, Tom."

"Shut up," Tom snapped. They walked in absolute silence about a block to the car. In that silence, numerous thoughts cascaded through his head.

His lip was huge, and the blood was still dripping. It would certainly be visible when he got up the next morning. He could visualize himself going to the kitchen. His older and younger brothers would see his huge lip and say, "What happened to you?" He would look at them and say . . . nothing. They would know that someone had beaten him up and gotten the best of him. He would have to tell them that he had done nothing about it. They would look at him in silence, followed by a few questions as they tried to understand why he wouldn't stick up for himself. Any respect they had for him would be lost, and more importantly, he knew his own self-respect would be seriously damaged. He couldn't tolerate that. That idea was more painful than anything he had faced a few minutes earlier.

After several minutes of silence, Tom said, "I've got to go back."

Jeff was elated. "You gotta kick this guy to a pulp," he urged.

"Shut up, Jeff. You don't say a word." Tom was still very scared. "All I'm going to do is go back and make him apologize." After saying it, he realized how ridiculous it was.

He was going to be in a fight and didn't know how his opponent's gang buddies were going to respond.

As he and Jeff walked up the driveway, he saw them standing in the same spot they were in before. The guy who had hit him seemed to be in a great mood, apparently eating up the attention he was receiving for beating up a white boy. One of his friends saw Tom and tapped his friend on the shoulder and pointed. When the guy saw Tom, his eyes lit up. He seemed to be pleased that he was going to get another opportunity.

Tom's senses were very alert. Maybe it was his fear or his adrenaline kicking in, but he noticed everything. Things seemed to move more slowly. Tom was not only watching his attacker, but he noticed what his friends were doing and what others around them were doing.

Soon, Tom was face-to-face with his antagonist and said, "You like hitting people when they're not looking? How do you do when they're paying attention?"

"You want some more, white boy?" he taunted. "Come on." He put his fists up and took a wild swing at Tom with his right hand.

Tom couldn't believe how slow the guy was. Ducking out of the way, Tom threw three quick punches, two of which connected with his face. The third missed as he moved back. As the guy stood upright, Tom threw another, connecting square on the jaw. His adrenaline was working overtime. He felt no fear. He was tightly focused on his aggression. He hit the guy again.

Sensing he had no chance standing toe-to-toe with Tom, the guy put his head down and charged like a wrestler. Tom stepped aside, grabbed the back of his neck, and slammed him to the ground. He jumped on the guy and began delivering body shots and shots to the head as his opponent covered his face with both arms.

"You like hitting someone who's not looking?" Tom said, spewing profanities. "How about now? Get up! Is this all you've got?"

The guy was hurt pretty bad and wasn't fighting back, so Tom kicked him, backed off, and started yelling at his friends. "You guys want some, too? Come on, I'll reshape all your ugly faces."

Tom didn't feel like himself. He could see that the guy's friends were nervous and scared. They probably thought he was a crazy man. He was jumping around with the attitude that he would whip all of them, and he told them so. While he challenged the friends, the guy on the ground painfully and slowly stood up. His face, his bearing, and his whole body clearly said that he'd had enough. He began slowly moving toward the house.

A guy came up to Tom and said, "You'd better get out of out of here quick. He just went to the house to get a gun."

Tom and Jeff ran down the driveway and all the way to the car. His adrenaline was still pumping. All sense of fear was gone.

~~~

Tom was quiet now. No one spoke. Three wide-open eyes were fixed on him. He remembered that he had never told his wife about this event from his youth.

Looking at each member of his family, he said, "I wanted to tell you about that event. I know it was traumatic. I could never forget it, because I learned some important things about myself that I would remember for the rest of my life. My fears prevented me from taking action. Only when I realized that taking no action would injure my self-esteem did I overcome the fear of more injuries. The result was that I acted, even though I was terrified. I learned that all of us have something very powerful inside of us that goes untapped until we force ourselves to call upon it. It is an internal power, which, once unleashed, will allow us to do things we never believed we were capable of. We've seen many people in history who have found this gift and done extraordinary things, but many go through life never realizing what lies inside
~~~

them. I found out there was something inside of me. Later in my life, I discovered that it is a gift from God that He wants us to use."

The room remained silent for a long moment while his family grappled with the reality that the man they were looking at could have been killed before he ever became a husband and father. Tom looked at the ceiling, and in his mind's eye saw the plaque on the wall of his business office: *With God, all things are possible.*

Nervously scratching his cheek, Johnny said, "That was scary, Dad."

Lonnie, holding her chin in the palms of her hand, said almost in a whisper, "You could have been killed."

Tom slowly nodded.

"No, hon, you hadn't told me that story before," said Janelle. "Now I know why you give those motivational speeches so persuasively."

Tom smiled appreciatively.

"Hey, Dad, you've got to tell us about the miracle that changed your life," piped up Johnny. "You promised."

"I know, Johnny. Thanks for reminding me. It's hard for me to talk about. Give me a couple minutes to think about it."

He stood and walked to the large picture window in the front room. Unfocused, he stared into the distance. He thought about the days of his youth as he gazed out over the frozen, snow-covered lake. It was still snowing, with large snowflakes gently falling earthward, covering everything in a soft blanket of fluffy whiteness. He marveled at the amazing construction of each snowflake. Like people, each one was different from the other. But unlike people, each flake was pure and perfect.

During the years of his youth, he had done many things he wasn't proud of. He had heard about a God but had no connection with Him. Now he did. As he gazed at the winter scenery, Isaiah 1:18 floated through his mind: *Though your sins be as scarlet, they shall be as white as snow.*

He looked up into the millions of descending snowflakes and uttered a silent prayer of gratitude. Turning back to his family, he began his story.

~~~

It was the summer of his high school graduation. He felt a certain amount of pressure to decide what he was going to do, but he was also having a lot of fun. He had gotten a job at McDonald's. The owner owned several in the area and sponsored a McDonald's basketball team. One reason he liked Tom was because he was one of the best players on the basketball team. The team won trophies and gained valuable publicity. Tom was soon promoted to store manager.

Making money as a manager of a McDonald's restaurant and living at home with virtually no expenses, his life was good. He took the closing job at McDonald's so he could have the day to surf and have fun with friends.

One night, after he had closed the store, some friends met him at his house. It was about 1:00 a.m., and at eighteen years old, they were in his bedroom, drinking beer and smoking pot. His stepfather was home, but he was indifferent to these kinds of activities. Marijuana's primary effect, Tom knew, was to loosen up the users and rid them of their inhibitions. It made women vulnerable to men seeking to take advantage of them, and made anyone more prone to do dumb or illegal things.

The discussion was light until his two "friends," who had obviously spent time planning the conversation, unveiled their plan to rob the McDonald's store with his help. As a store manager, Tom had the keys to the door and the combination for the safe. He understood how the security system worked and knew when the deposits went to the bank and on what days the deposits would be doubled up and likely to be highest.

At first, he thought they were joking, but soon it became clear that it wasn't a joke. As soon as he realized they
~~~

were serious, he froze.

At the time, his religious background was extremely limited. He had been dragged to church a few times by his grandparents when he was young, but had never connected to God. He was agnostic at best and never had any real spiritual awareness. He had never prayed or looked to God for anything. He was responsible for himself. He was the master of his fate.

At that moment, however, he felt a strong and unmistakable dark presence in his bedroom. There was no voice, just a clear presence. Looking at his friends, he saw it in them and felt it all around him. It was evil, and it terrified him.

He jumped up and, in front of his friends, said, “God, please help. I need You with me. Please come into my room now.”

As clearly as he had felt and seen that unmistakable dark presence in his room just minutes earlier, his mind’s eye now clearly saw a brilliant light.

Tom felt strongly that he was at a fork in the road of his life. He had a choice. He could choose a life of drugs, crime, and jails – or something new and different. Utter darkness waited on one side, and brilliant light on the other.

It was a clear answer from God. He placed his hands on Tom that night, and Tom knew He would never let him go.

Tom quickly told his friends they needed to leave. He didn’t care about being embarrassed. Something was going on that was scary and he couldn’t explain. But deep down, he knew what it was.

He escorted his friends to the front door. After letting them out, he went into the living room, turned on all the lights, got down on his knees, and began praying to God. He cried and prayed until early in the morning. He didn’t sleep that night.

The next day, nothing was clearer to him than that the drugs made him vulnerable to evil forces, and he had to get out of California. That day, he left California for Washington

State. He had no functioning family to say goodbye to or get permission from. After the spiritual awakening that had taken place, he felt he was being called to a new life. Or, more importantly, he felt he was being warned to abandon the life he was living. He was determined that his future actions would be positive. He knew now that he was a servant of his Creator.

~~~

Once again, Tom looked around at the wide eyes of his beloved children, who had followed the story with anticipation. He stood up and walked around the table to his wife. They hugged, both with tears in their eyes.

"Thank you, sweetheart," he said to her. "Thank you for believing in me and helping me. I couldn't have done it without you."

Both his children approached. Together they got a tight bear hug that almost hurt.

"You are our precious children," said Tom. "We love you more than we can ever express. I'm so grateful that your youth is so different from mine. I'm grateful not just for where I am and how happy I am, but I believe because of my background, I'm a better father, husband, and person. I have strong empathy for people in less-than-desirable circumstances, but I also have unwavering confidence that with the help of God, anyone can change their circumstances if they are committed to doing so."

Looking into his children's eyes, he saw a glimmer of that vulnerable child who had put his trust in God many years ago.

With God, all things are possible.
— Matthew 19:26

~~~

When Death Conquers the Will to Live

Joe Moser sat on the front patio of his home in Ferndale, Washington, soaking up the sun. It was a beautiful day in the Pacific Northwest. The tall fir trees surrounding the yard swayed gently in the breeze. The sweet scent of summer hung richly in the air, and Joe inhaled deeply.

His five children sat in lawn chairs around the table, finishing the lunch their mother had made for them on this Saturday afternoon.

His son's voice broke the momentary silence. "Dad, somebody told me that you were a fighter pilot during the war."

Joe Jr.'s question struck him like a bolt out of the blue. Somewhat bewildered, Joe looked into his twelve-year-old son's brown eyes, wide with curiosity. His question seemed to have captured the attention of his siblings, and they all turned to stare at their father.

"You never told us about being in the war," Joe Jr. continued. "Why did you become a fighter pilot?"

Joe was not in the habit of talking about his wartime experiences. He had not even told his wife all that had happened to him; he certainly didn't want to tell his young children. He would never want them to know the cruelty their father had experienced at the hands of fellow human beings. He also knew, looking at the eager faces of his children, that he wouldn't be able to ignore his son's question.

He took a deep breath and straightened in his chair, thinking back on that time so many years ago. "Okay, Joe. I'll tell you why I became a fighter pilot. As a kid, I loved looking at airplanes. Maybe it was because I often saw planes on landing approach to Bellingham airport. Of course, no airlines were flying into Bellingham in the 1930s. Only small private planes. Our family farm was close to the final-approach flight path. I even bought a subscription to an aviation magazine. In one of those magazines, I saw a picture of what was then an experimental fighter plane. And when I saw a picture of what looked like a fierce flying fighting machine, I was smitten. It had two powerful engines, a long horizontal stabilizer, including the elevator connected to twin tail booms, and the two rounded tail rudders. I knew I wanted to fly that machine. It was the Lockheed P-38 Lightning."

His children all listened attentively. Even the youngest, Jolene, sat quietly.

"How did you get in the Air Force?" asked Joe Jr., already thinking ahead of his father's story.

"Well, at that time it was known as the U.S. Army Air Corps," Joe responded, "and it wasn't easy to get in. I didn't have the required two years of college and had pretty much given up hope. But then it was December 7, 1941, and the infamous Japanese sneak attack on Pearl Harbor. The mood of pacifism in the U.S. instantly changed to anger, and we were involved in World War II. I wanted to serve my country and was sworn in as a member of the Army Air Corps on May 18, 1942."

"Can you tell us about your pilot training?" asked his oldest, Janet. With her long dark hair and expressive eyes, she reminded Joe of his wife when she was younger.

"I went to California for training," Joe answered. "After about ten hours of dual instruction, I was supposed to be ready to solo, but my instructor said I was too 'mechanical' in my flying and he was going to 'wash me out' of the training program. I was devastated. All my dreams of flying the P-38 forever washed away. Imagine my surprise when my instructor told me the following day that he was going to give me one more chance. I was nervous but elated.

"We taxied to the take-off position when my instructor opened his door and said, 'Okay, Joe. Do a couple of take-offs and landings. You're on your own.'

"I must have looked at him with my mouth hanging open. I was more nervous and scared than a rabbit being eyed by a hungry bulldog. I knew my instructor was watching, and panic was not an option. I pushed the throttle of the single-engine tail-wheel trainer to the firewall and roared down the runway into the blue yonder. A few minutes later, I lined up on the final approach to the runway. The airplane was drifting to the left, and I needed to make corrections to counteract a brisk crosswind from the right. I was a bundle of nervous concentration. I held my breath until moments later, the two main wheels gently touched down right on the runway center-line. Keeping the tail wheel off the runway, I pushed the throttle to full power and lifted into the air again.

"Now, feeling mighty proud of my first solo takeoff and landing, I exhaled and began to relax. I caught a glimpse of my instructor as he was watching me. *Wow, he must be impressed with my perfect first solo performance*, I thought. 'Too mechanical in my flying,' he had said. What a bunch of malarkey! He was probably embarrassed now watching me fly solo with perfection for the first time.

"Now I was lining up with the runway again. This time I would make a full-stop landing. Again the main wheels and tires squeaked onto the runway. It was music to my ears. Gradually the airplane lost speed, and the tail wheel settled onto the asphalt. That's when the crosswind came to bite me. I wasn't quick enough on the rudder pedals to steer the nose wheel. The wind caught my right wing, and in a flash, the airplane swiveled around in a near-360-degree turn called a ground loop, but I managed to keep the wing tip from scraping the runway and damaging the plane. Nevertheless, from that day on, all my fellow cadets called me Ground Loop Joe."

Smiling at the memory, Joc turned his eyes to the cloudless sky above, where he had spent so much time during those days. For a moment, his thoughts wandered to the many times he had come so incredibly close to death . . . even the time death had conquered his will to live. So many times that he could not have imagined he would ever experience being surrounded by a loving family sitting around him on lawn chairs. With a heart overflowing with gratitude, he looked at each of them in turn.

He could tell that sixteen-year-old Janet wanted to ask him a question.

"Dad," she said, "did you ever have anything funny or really scary happen while you were training?"

Joe stared pensively at a lonely dandelion flower in the middle of his lawn. Then he started laughing. "You know, kids," he started, "when a student pilot gets into something really dangerous, it usually turns into something very funny, provided it doesn't kill the student pilot. As my training progressed, it became increasingly intensive, and the trainer aircraft increasingly more sophisticated. I completely understood. They were preparing us for combat with enemy aircraft that had only one focus. That focus would be to knock my aircraft out of the sky and kill me. I was being trained how to avoid becoming an easy enemy target, and at the same time how to gain a tactical advantage over any enemy aircraft.

"My training aircraft was the Ryan PT-22. It was an open-cockpit airplane, with the instructor sitting in the rear seat. During steep corkscrew climbs and screaming near-vertical dives and all other wild training maneuvers, both cadet and instructor were supposed to be firmly harnessed to their seats. When the instructor barked into the headphones to do a horizontal roll, the student had better comply – and I did.

"When my instructor remained silent after the roll maneuver, I figured it probably meant to do another roll. Still no new instructions likely meant another upside-down, right-side-up maneuver was to be repeated. But a quick glimpse into the backseat immediately explained the reason the headphones had remained silent. My instructor had fallen out of the upside-down airplane. He had forgotten to fasten his harness, and away he went. Since he saved his life by pulling his parachute ripcord, a very dangerous occurrence turned into a big, funny joke."

As Joe looked at his son and daughters with their wide-eyed expressions, something told him that they didn't think it was funny.

"Good grief," said Joyce, who at thirteen sounded just like her mother. "I can't think of anything scarier than falling out of an upside-down airplane. Even with a parachute, I'm pretty sure I would have soiled my shorts."

Joe laughed and nodded agreeably. That comment from Joyce immediately reminded him of another flying incident. "Yes, kids, I'll tell you about the time I wished I could have soiled my shorts instead of doing what I did."

The kids responded almost in unison: "What did you do, Dad?"

He raised his eyebrows. "Are you sure you want to know? It was very dangerous and very 'yuck.'"

"Okay, Dad, whatever," said Janet. "You've got us curious now. Just tell us."

Joe cleared his throat and gazed at the tree line a short distance away. A slight smile curled his mouth as the memories of long ago became clear in his mind again.

"On October 1, 1943, I and my forty-seven classmates became commissioned officers, second lieutenants, in the U.S. Army Air Corps. That didn't mean the end of our training. We transitioned to increasingly more powerful and sophisticated flying machines. Finally I climbed into the cockpit of my young boyhood dreams, the powerful twin-engine P-38

Lightning. The cockpit of the P-38 is very small. Fortunately, I was not a six-foot, two-hundred-pounds-plus pilot. I had received my twin-engine training in an aircraft with a seat for the instructor pilot. The P-38 barely had space for one pilot. When I first squeezed myself into the pilot seat of the P-38, I looked at the array of instruments in awe.

"As I pushed the twin throttles briskly forward to full take-off power, I knew I was living the fulfillment of a dream. We knew we were being prepared for air combat. We knew that our adversaries might be much more experienced, and our instructors did everything in their power to prepare us for survival, even if we were to go up against the best aces of the German Luftwaffe, or air force. All the training maneuvers were designed to help us gain confidence in our abilities and become the best-trained, safest fighter pilots possible.

"This intensive training was not without peril, which was made painfully clear to us when two of our fellow cadets collided on a training mission. Both of them died. We had been training together for almost two years and had become close friends. Their loss was very painful. As young, hotshot pilots, we had a feeling of invulnerability. Yet we knew we were being prepared for combat and that death would never be far away."

He glanced at his children. Their faces were pale, their eyes worried.

Eight-year-old Julie took advantage of his pause and said, "Dad, I think I'm going to throw up."

"Oh no, don't do that," responded Joe. "I'm just ready to get to the funny part."

Now he had their attention again. Their revolted expressions disappeared from their faces, and he could tell they were curious to learn what happened next.

"During this training run, my wingmen and I were already in the air when I began to feel sick. I think it was a bad combination of the altitude and the sauerkraut I had for lunch. In order to get my head between my knees in the tiny cockpit,

I had to push the control stick forward – which sent the airplane into a very steep dive. Of course, my two wingmen had no choice but to follow me. They knew that this was not the area where we had been ordered to practice our simulated combat mission, but in the military, discipline is discipline. It is never to be compromised. They followed my dive without having any idea what precipitated it. Their two-year experience had never given them the impression that their buddy Joe was not a good, serious, perfection-oriented pilot, but this was nuts. They were yelling into their microphones: 'Joe, are you okay?'

"Of course, I couldn't hear them. Just as I was pulling the control stick back to put the airplane in a climb, as well as getting my oxygen mask in place, I realized my stomach convulsions weren't finished yet. I knew that at 18,000 feet, I would not be able to remain conscious for long without oxygen.

"Four times, we went into a steep dive before my stomach was empty and the sausages and sauerkraut were on the floor of the airplane. I was very conscious of the fact that the San Bernardino mountaintops were filling my windshield and rushing up to meet us. I started pulling out of the dive and getting my headphones and oxygen mask in place again. One quick glance confirmed that my two wingmen were right on my tail. I took a deep drag of pure oxygen and placed the headphones over my ears.

"They were frantically yelling into their microphones: 'Joe, what's wrong with you?' I'm sure they fully expected me to go into another dive just like the previous four. They knew that the fifth one would be the last one. If they continued to follow me, they too would collide violently with a mountaintop, which would mean instant death. Maybe they were contemplating the question of discipline versus death.

"Fortunately, they didn't have to make that momentous decision. My microphone was in place again, and I told them that we would abandon the planned mission and return to base, and I would show them what happened. I could tell that they were very curious, though still shaky.

"After we landed, they came running to my airplane. I had already slid my canopy cover back, and they each jumped onto a wing and put their heads inside my cockpit. If it is possible to faint and still remain fully conscious, that would describe my two wingmen. One eyeful and one noseful practically made them fall off the wings. Then they relaxed and released all their pent-up fears and tensions by laughing uproariously.

"Two guys from the ground crew came up to my plane and asked if they could do anything for me. I nodded my head, and they jumped on the wing. I said, 'I need my cockpit cleaned up.'

"They both took one look and one whiff and said, 'Sorry, pilot, you clean that up yourself.' So that's what I did."

His children's serious expressions told Joe that they didn't find the story very funny. They seemed less focused on the comical aspect and more on the hazards their father had experienced in his youthful pursuit of becoming a fighter pilot. He decided for certain that they were far too young to absorb the horrors he had experienced when his brief military career as a fighter pilot had suddenly crashed.

"Dad, do you have any more wartime stories?" asked Joe Jr., the worry clearing from his eyes.

The other kids all nodded, with a chorus of yeses. Janet twirled a strand of hair between her fingers as she awaited the next story. Julie clutched her knees to her chest with excitement.

"Okay, kids, let me think for a minute." Joe watched a robin work hard to extract a worm out of the lawn. She must have had quite a few baby robins to feed, Joe thought, because she didn't fly away until she had several worms in her beak. The robin remained constantly alert, swiveling her head and looking in every direction.

That reminded Joe of his fighter pilot days. He turned back to look at his children. "On April 25, 1944, I was stationed on my base in England and flew my first successful mission. It was only a short hop to cross the North Sea and be over the western European coastline and enemy territory.

"I could hardly believe that my boyhood dreams had come true. Here I was, piloting the fastest, most advanced fighter plane in the world. It had performed incredibly well in Africa by virtually destroying the supply lines to the advancing German armies. The P-38 was primarily responsible for breaking the back of German General Rommel's advances in Africa. It was both hated and feared by the Germans, who called the P-38 the Fork-Tailed Devil.

"I spotted a couple of what appeared to be military trucks on a highway in Holland. Here we go, I thought. This is for real. Flying at 18,000 feet, I continued heading east before making a 180-degree turn. Now I had the sun behind me and I would be harder to spot. As I dove for my target, a haunting thought flashed through my mind. Was this the first time in my life that I was going to kill some fellow human beings? That was totally foreign to my nature. I couldn't even kill an animal. The targets loomed rapidly larger in my 50-millimeter machine gun sight. This was war. This was what I was trained for. I hadn't started this war, and I wanted to help end it.

"Moments later, I left three completely destroyed German military trucks in flames as I climbed up to altitude and headed west across the North Sea back to base."

"Wow!" exclaimed Joe Jr. The girls exchanged glances, some solemn, others thrilled.

Joe swatted at a fly that had landed on his forehead. Then he looked up at the cloudless blue sky. His mind had already formed very clear scenes of what he would tell his children next. They were young, and he knew that they would not yet fully understand the gravity of the dangers he had faced every day. They wouldn't be able to form a concept of sitting between two powerful engines in a very confined cockpit, flying at 25,000 feet without heat in the cockpit, with temperatures ranging from minus-twenty to sometimes as low as minus-seventy degrees.

"Do you have another war story, Dad?" asked Joyce.

He nodded. "I have two more I'll tell you, if you want to hear them."

They all nodded enthusiastically.

"Okay. This happened on May 13, 1944. We were to meet up with a large group of B-17s when they were returning from a daytime bombing raid on Berlin. We were to intercept them over the Baltic Sea not far from Sweden and provide escort as they returned to their base in England. Those B-17s that had been damaged to some degree by German anti-aircraft fire were especially vulnerable to German scavenger fighter planes. The German Luftwaffe didn't rule the skies over Western Europe anymore. Incessant bombing by the Allies had destroyed much of their manufacturing and supply capacity. And the superbly trained Allied fighter pilots had dramatically diminished the ranks of German ace pilots. That's why a crippled bomber made attractive prey for rookie German fighter pilots.

"We met up with the formations of returning B-17s over Denmark. We were flying at 25,000 feet, which was 5,000 feet above the bombers. This protected the bombers from diving attacks from above by German fighters. Unfortunately, we could not provide protection from 88-millimeter shells the Germans fired at the bombers. They had programmed their projectiles to explode at 20,000 feet. When they calculated that our P-38s were at an altitude 5,000 feet higher, it was soon apparent that their shells were also programmed to explode at our altitude.

"Our planes were soon experiencing severe turbulence as the German shells exploded nearby. When encountering this situation, we had been trained to break formation so we wouldn't be such easy targets, and scatter in various directions. I banked sharply to the right, went into a steep dive, and soon found myself out of the heavy anti-aircraft flak area. The plan now was to regroup with our squadron and continue our mission of protecting our bomber friends from being attacked by diving German fighters. No matter how I searched, I was unable to locate any of my squadron. I was alone and feeling very uncomfortable.

"Instantly, my senses were in 'full alert' mode. I kept scanning the skies in every direction. I knew that a single fighter made a much more attractive victim for a pair of German fighters than a formation. Just as I was trained to come diving out of the sun to attack my prey, this was the German fighter pilot's strategy as well. I climbed to gain altitude, did an occasional three-sixty –"

"What's a three-sixty?" Julie asked.

"Oh, sure, I almost forgot you kids aren't pilots. A three-sixty is a complete three-hundred-sixty-degree turn. Which means that after completing the three-sixty, I'd be heading in the same direction I was heading before entering the turn. I did that to look for possible enemy fighters, as well as search for any member of our scattered squadron. Fortunately, I saw no enemy fighters, but I didn't see any of my buddies, either. It was not a situation I wanted to be in. I was anxious and kept turning my head, scanning the skies. Unfortunately, my head didn't even come close to having the swivel range of an owl. I kept repeating an occasional three-sixty while heading my plane in the direction of my base in England.

"Suddenly, way below my altitude, I spotted something very familiar. The outline of a B-17 bomber. It was just heading over the North Sea. I noticed smoke trailing from the heavy bomber. Here was a perfect target for a German fighter plane looking for an opportunity to score a 'kill.' Suddenly, all nervousness and anxiety left me. I had a mission. I could protect the lives of probably ten to twelve fellow Americans representing the crew of this injured B-17.

"I began my descent to join the bomber in a way that they would be able to see my approach. I knew they would rejoice when they saw the unmistakable outline of my P-38. It greatly improved their chances of survival. They knew there were no German fighter pilots remaining who would want to tangle with the feared American Lightning.

"The B-17 was crippling along on two engines at about 200 miles per hour and losing altitude. I needed to keep my speed up to no less than 300 miles per hour in case I would suddenly have to go on the attack to guard the B-17. I circled above the bomber and made lazy S-turns to stay close. The crew would certainly know that whoever the pilot was, he had no intention of forsaking his guardian role. Constantly losing altitude, they were increasingly at risk of having to ditch in the waters of the North Sea. I repeatedly attempted to contact them by radio. Since there was no response, I had to assume that their radio equipment was out of commission. Continuing to circle, making large figure-eight turns, I watched for enemy aircraft. But two other hazards worried me: my own dwindling fuel supply, and the B-17 sinking into the sea.

"Once more, I looked at the ever-decreasing altitude of the bomber. Then I saw the crew begin to jettison everything out through the open hatches that was not needed to keep the aircraft flying. Machine guns, ammunition, flight cases with maps, flight jackets, headphones, heavy boots, anything to lighten the load and reduce their rate of descent.

"To make a long story shorter, they thankfully made it back to their base. I didn't actually see them land, because my two engines were running on fumes and I had to scoot over to my base at Warmwell, which was southwest of London. I'm sure the crew of that stricken B-17, if they survived the war, would never forget the sudden appearance of a guardian angel who kept them safe from a sudden attack by enemy fighter planes."

Joe paused and gazed into the clear blue sky. "You know, kids, in my wildest dreams, I could not have imagined that so many years later I would meet a man who was a crew member of that B-17 bomber I escorted back to its base. It happened at a church gathering at my home church in Ferndale. Many members from other churches in the area joined in the annual summer barbeque event.

"I recognized a good-sized man named Earl who had joined in our church summer event a few times before. Earl was in an animated conversation with others sitting at the same table. I was close and began listening to Earl's conversation. I really tuned in sharply when I heard Earl starting to talk about his experiences during World War II.

"'We were flying from a long mission over Berlin,' Earl said. 'We had two of our four engines shot out by flak over Denmark, and I thought we were never going to make it back. We were simply sitting ducks for a German fighter. Easy prey. I was waiting and watching for some lonely fighter to hit us and finish us off any minute. I was sure May 13, 1944, would be the day and year I would die. Suddenly, I saw this plane up above and behind us, and I thought, here it is, the end. I didn't think I'd have enough time to swivel my machine gun in the direction of the bogey.

"'I looked again and yelled to my fellow crew members, "Hey, guys, it's a friendly. It's a P-38. It's one of ours." Oh, man, I can't tell you how relieved I was at the welcome sight of a P-38 fighter plane. That guy followed us all the way back to England. He was doing figure-eights to stay with our much slower damaged B-17. That pilot was our protector. He saved our lives. I'm sure of it. He may not have survived the war, but if by some miracle I should ever meet him, I'd want to embrace him long and tight.'

"I listened to Earl and realized that I remembered that event very well. I couldn't stand it anymore. I stood up, reached out my hand to Earl, and quietly said, 'Earl, I was that pilot.'

"Earl's eyes grew large as an expression of incredulity came over his face. He jumped from his chair, and this big man embraced me in a long, tight bear hug while mumbling endless thank-yous. Tears welled up in our eyes. We remained lifelong friends."

~~~

The front door opened, and Joe's wife, Jean, appeared with a tray of glasses filled with lemonade. A chorus of jubilation from her children greeted her.

"Wow, Mom, thanks a lot," said Julie. "This'll taste so good today. It's so warm outside." The others all agreed.

"Dad is telling some scary stories about the war," Joe Jr. informed their mother.

Jean looked at Joe with a smile, her eyes sparkling behind her glasses. "I'm so happy that his life was spared," she said, "that he came back, and that we were married and have the happiest little family in the world."

Joe and Jean exchanged a long glance and then looked admiringly at their offspring as the children enjoyed the refreshing lemonade.

"Okay, Dad," said Joe Jr. "You said you were going to tell us one more fighter pilot story."

"You're right," said Joe. "I'll tell you about my forty-fourth and final mission of the war."

"Was that the end of the war, then?"

"No, son, that wasn't the end of the war. For me, it was the beginning of something so horrible that I never talk about it to anybody. Maybe when you kids are older and I'm older and my nightmares gradually go away, I'll tell you the rest of my Second World War experiences."

Jean settled into a lawn chair as the children leaned forward with curiosity. Joe quickly launched into the recollections of his final mission of the war in his P-38 Lightning.

"August 13, 1944, was a hot day in France, where our squadron had been relocated to a hastily improvised base with a steel-matted runway. On June 6, Allied forces had landed on the beaches of Normandy. While sustaining heavy losses, they had nevertheless gained a foothold on the mainland of
~~~

Europe. The Germans were rapidly sending more manpower and equipment to the front lines, and for some time had succeeded in fighting the Allied invasion forces to a standstill. Now our ground forces were making rapid progress on their way to liberate Paris and France. Our orders were to destroy anything that moved on the roads. The Germans were frantically trying to resupply their retreating forces. It was our job to inflict maximum damage to their efforts.

"On this hot, hazy day, the visibility was limited. I was the wing leader with the code name Censor Red. My wingman was flying slightly behind and to my right. He was to follow my every move and look for and protect me from possible attacking enemy aircraft. I looked intently for targets from 4,000 feet in the air.

"Suddenly, I activated my microphone and excitedly announced to my wingman, 'Censor Red Leader, truck convoy on road. I'm diving in for the attack.'

"My P-38 screamed toward my target at over 400 miles per hour. The target loomed larger in my windshield, and my finger was on the bomb-release switch. Before I could release my bombs, I felt a tremendous shudder as flak exploded all around me. A large-caliber shell had destroyed my left engine and set it ablaze."

The kids looked at him wide-eyed, fear reflected in their faces. "What did you do?" Julie asked.

"I tried to climb and get back and out of enemy-controlled airspace, but the fire kept growing and would soon be in the cockpit. I knew that many pilots had died burning up in their cockpits. I pulled the canopy release, and as it blew away, a wave of hot air hit me. I had to get out of my fatally damaged airplane. I flipped the P-38 upside down, while at the same time unbuckling my harness. I fell out.

"We had been briefed repeatedly that the most serious hazard while bailing out of a P-38 was slamming into the airplane's tail. Immediately I glued my eyes to the horizontal stabilizer between the two tail booms. Because I was so intent on avoiding a fatal collision with the tail section, I hadn't noticed that the toe of my boot had caught in the canopy rail and I was being dragged at nearly 400 miles per hour to a violent death on French soil. I prayed very hard as I saw the earth rushing up to meet me. Just as I realized that in the next two seconds I would die and meet my maker, my boot tore loose. I jerked the ripcord. A terrific jolt told me that my parachute had deployed.

"The next instant, I hit the ground hard. I was stunned and suddenly realized that I was not in friendly territory. In spite of my valiant efforts and the help of some patriotic Frenchmen to help me escape, I was captured."

Joe stopped. He raised his head slightly and looked at his children, who all stared at their father.

Julie was the first to speak. "Wasn't it a miracle that you survived?"

Joe simply nodded.

"What happened after you were captured?" Joe Jr. asked.

Preoccupied by thoughts of that terrible time, Joe stared down at his hands, taking a few moments before he answered. "When all this happened, I wasn't much older than you all are now. Just a few short years. I've never been able to talk about the events and suffering that happened after my capture. I've never even told your mom. Maybe I'll be able to tell you when you're older. It's too painful."

He turned his gaze once again to the blue skies above and started getting up from his chair. "Too painful," he repeated, laying a hand on his son's shoulder. Tears moistened his eyes as he silently walked to the house. Despite the beautiful day and the pleasant presence of his family, he suddenly needed to be alone.

~~~

Many years later, on a Friday afternoon, Joe lay on his back in a small, dark basement room, pointing a flashlight at the innards of a furnace. In all the years he had been a furnace
~~~

repair specialist, he could not recall a single time that he had failed to correctly diagnose a furnace problem.

But this was a very old model he had never encountered before. The factory operating manuals had long been lost. Nevertheless, Joe was not worried. He knew furnaces inside and out, and he'd already identified the defective part, which he knew wasn't available anymore. His challenge was to figure out an unconventional way to repair this problem. He would return to the shop, apply his creativity, and come up with a solution.

He checked his watch as he ascended the stairs and discovered that it was nearly six o'clock. In the customer's kitchen, where the lady of the house was preparing the evening meal, he explained the problem with the furnace and assured her that he would be back to work on the problem on Saturday.

The next day, Joe's creative resolution to the unusual furnace problem worked perfectly, and he drove leisurely down I-5 back toward home in Ferndale, feeling a sense of satisfaction. His thoughts wandered now as he counted all the blessings in his life. He could never have married anyone better than his wife, Jean. She was a fantastic mother for his children and now an equally fantastic grandmother. *The incredible blessings of a most fulfilling life,* he thought.

He found himself once again recalling the day in 1944 when he had died. Each day since then had truly been a miracle.

A new thought jolted him, and he suddenly turned the wheel, taking the Bakerview Road exit toward the Bellingham airport. He parked his car near the FedEx offices and headed for runway 16. The fall air was chilly, but the sun shone. He unzipped his jacket as he walked.

What had jolted him was the promise he had made to his children when they were much younger, that someday he would tell them about the events that had happened to him after he was captured by the Germans on August 13, 1944. He had promised them that he would relate the rest of his wartime experiences when they were older. He wanted to forget that promise, but he knew that his grown children would not let him forget. As painful as it would be to bring all those horrible memories to the surface again, he knew he had better mentally prepare for it.

He sat down in the grass not far from the edge of the active runway and let his mind drift back to the days, weeks, and months after his capture in a part of France that was still occupied by the German armies.

~~~

He could never forget the hellish train journey he had spent packed tightly in a cattle railroad car. It was the first time he had experienced the fact that human beings were capable of treating their fellow humans worse than animals. In the eyes of the German guards, his life had no more value than the life of a pesky fly.

During the course of that unspeakable train ride, he and his fellow soldiers became totally dehumanized. Without water, food, or sanitary facilities, many of them died. Joe had a strong will to live. He wanted to see his family and loved ones again. After surviving forty-three missions as a fighter pilot over enemy territory, he didn't want to die now.

They were being taken to a prisoner-of-war camp. Treatment would surely be more humane than the horrors of the train ride in a cattle car.

When they finally arrived at their destination in the dark heart of Nazi Germany, the soldiers did not find the POW camp they had expected. Instead, they had arrived at the notorious, torturous death camp known as Buchenwald. Exiting the cattle car, which he had endured for five long days, Joe and his fellow captured soldiers stumbled along a narrow path between two rows of SS guards, each holding the leash of a powerful German shepherd dog. Each dog strained at the leash, growling angrily with teeth bared, ready to rip them apart.
~~~

They entered the camp through a secondary gate. Joe saw a chimney spewing thick black smoke into the air. He did not know that the odor he smelled and the smoke he saw came from burning human flesh.

One of the German guards spoke a little English as they walked past the building with the smoking chimney. "None of you will leave this camp except as smoke coming from that chimney," he said with a leering smile.

Then Joe knew it was a crematorium. He knew that this was not a prisoner-of-war camp, but something far worse than any of them could have imagined. It was a place where prisoners were worked to death, starved to death, executed, and burned.

~~~

Joe's thoughts were interrupted by the sound of airplane engines. He scanned the sky and spotted a twin-engine jet on the downwind leg of its landing approach. He watched it make a right turn, followed soon by another right turn to final approach for landing on runway 16.

He'd never lost his love and admiration for those amazing flying machines. He watched intently as the speedy private jet crossed the runway threshold, and seconds later he heard that sweet chirping sound as the wheels and tires were suddenly required to begin rotating at over 100 mph. He followed the jet's progress as it applied reverse thrust power and taxied to the terminal.

Again he scanned the sky surrounding the airport and observed a small aircraft approaching from the west at a 45-degree angle. As it turned on final approach, he recognized it as a small, two-seat Cessna model 150 training plane. *Probably a student with instructor*, he thought. Judging from the small but abrupt variation of altitude and engine sound, he felt sure the pilot was a student. The plane was still twenty feet in the air when it crossed the landing threshold. It continued to descend until it suddenly dropped the last several feet of altitude, resulting in a solid bounce into the air, followed by
~~~

another bounce moments later. He could tell when the instructor took over applying full power and repeated the entire landing process.

He could sit there and watch airplanes all afternoon. It took all the willpower he could muster to return his thoughts to the indescribable miseries of Buchenwald.

~~~

He spent two months in the purgatory known as Buchenwald. He lost fifty pounds and his sense of self as a human being. The camp held 80,000 prisoners, including 168 Air Force officers and enlisted men. They were not criminals, terrorists, or members of the French resistance. They belonged in a prisoner-of-war camp, where they would be treated according to the rules of the Geneva Convention. As pilots, officers, and soldiers, they did not belong in Buchenwald, where they were treated worse than animals.

On October 12, 1944, the POWs were visited by high-ranking German Luftwaffe officers. How these officers came to know that many captured pilots and airmen were being held in a death camp, Joe never knew. On October 20, the POWS were loaded in railroad cars, and two days later they arrived in a POW camp known as Stalag 111 about 70 miles southeast of Berlin. This camp was specifically for captured Air Force officers.

Compared to Buchenwald, the food, clothing, and treatment they received in this new camp made it seem like paradise. Their fellow POWs simply could not believe them when they described their experiences in Buchenwald.

First they heard the artillery fire in the far distance, but each day the sound came closer. Russian forces were relentlessly advancing deeper into the German heartland. It was January 27, 1945, and Joe knew it wouldn't be long before the Russians would overrun Stalag 111. He had no idea what would await him. The weather had turned brutally cold, and he learned later that the winter of 1944-1945 was the coldest of the twentieth century.
~~~

Early on the morning of January 28, 1945, the POWs left Stalig 111 on foot for an unknown destination, farther away from the advancing Russians. They formed a single line, flanked by German guards, and started walking down the narrow, snow-covered road. The weather was brutal. They walked straight into the howling winds that swept up the snow and created whiteout blizzard conditions. The temperature dropped to 28 degrees below zero. Icy snow pelted their faces, and Joe knew they wouldn't be able to survive this for long.

There was no conversation. Together with his fellow prisoners, he continued to struggle forward, one step at a time, hour after torturous hour.

Joe was trudging behind Lt. Jenkins, a strong young man. He had been an all-American football player. At one point, Jenkins turned halfway around and said, "Joe, I want to die."

With that, he sank into the snow. He gave Joe what remained of his meager rations and died. His suffering was done.

Joe closed Jenkins' eyes, stepped over his lifeless body, and continued to place one foot in front of the other. Increasingly he had to step over lifeless bodies, which soon formed into clumps of icy snow.

~~~

Taking a deep breath, Joe tore his thoughts away from that deadly march. He thought about the young farm boy he had been from Ferndale, Washington, a young man full of life. Dreaming of pushing the throttles forward and feeling the powerful surge of the aircraft engines propelling him into the air. Playing hide-and-go-seek with fluffy clouds. Screaming down on enemy targets with guns blazing. That was the life he had planned.

The memories now flooded through his head with such intensity that he could almost feel one cold, painful, crunching step after another, crossing one frozen clump of flesh and
~~~

blood after another. He heard the sound of another airplane engine. This time he didn't even look up as the painful memories of the death march enveloped him.

No wonder he never wanted to talk about it. It was still too traumatic even to think about it. But he had promised his now grown children. He would never make a promise he couldn't or wouldn't keep. He forced his thoughts to return to the narrow, snowy, icy country roads deep in East Germany.

~~~

He came to another barely recognizable human form along the side of the road. Was it a pile of snow-covered rags? No, it was an American or English or Australian flyer. Another young man whose dreams of adventure, of a future, of love and a family, would never materialize. There might never even be a marble cross engraved with his name, the date of his birth, and the date of his death. It was far more likely that a wild animal would rip his remains apart, leaving only some bones. Will that soon be me? Joe wondered.

His strength was fading fast, his energies depleted. Yes, the end of his life was near. He could feel it. He was sure of it, and it would be okay. Then he thought of his family as he took another painful step. Would they ever find him? Would they ever know what had happened to him? The will to live made him put one foot after another, trudging on in frozen desolation along the narrow, winding roads. Each step became an act of will, of courage and tenacity. It was the will to live that kept him going even when all strength was quickly fading away.

Virtually without stopping, they had walked for nearly 27 hours and covered about 30 miles. Those who hadn't been starved in Buchenwald had more strength and energy than those who had experienced the horrors of the death camp.

During most of the day, Joe struggled to keep up. It was getting harder for him. Much harder.

Toward late afternoon, he started to feel better. He experienced a growing warmth inside and a feeling of well-
~~~

being. He was going home, and it felt so good. He could just lie down, and everything would be okay. His sense of peace and acceptance turned into a kind of euphoria. He didn't know it then, but death was conquering his will to live.

Peacefully, he sagged down in the snow, and all went dark.

He woke up in a small hospital in the village of Bad Muskau. He learned that two men following him had used what little energy they had left to drag his unconscious dead weight a quarter of a mile to the village.

For the rest of his life, he had regretted never knowing the names of his self-sacrificing guardian angels. He continued to harbor the hope that one or both of them might still be alive. Nothing would have given him greater joy than to be able to thank them for saving his life.

~~~

Joe Moser finally arrived home to reunite with his family on June 10, 1945. He married his beloved Jean on June 26, 1946. Together they raised a family of four daughters and a son, Joe Jr.

Joe's complete, detailed account of his wartime experiences is documented in his book, A Fighter Pilot in Buchenwald, *by Joseph F. Moser as told by Gerald R. Baron. This book is copyrighted in 2009 and can be ordered from Exxel Publishing Co.*
~~~

The Accident

by H. J. Baron

I feel at once that something is wrong. It's that feeling that steals inside your blood and chills it. It comes unbidden, not because something is badly out of place, and even before there's a sudden telephone call or someone isn't there when she should be. It comes when an internal signal calls the alert, before you know why.

I let my eyes wander over the crowd that was mostly seated already. We stand at the back of the chapel auditorium on the Christian Reformed Conference grounds right on Lake Michigan. Ruth and I had come from Grand Rapids, had met our friends at their nearby cottage, then came with them to take in the service, after which we planned to spend a leisurely evening together back at the cottage and the beach. Now I look hard. Someone should have been here by now. But she isn't.

~~~

Earlier that afternoon, still at home. It was a warm, lazy Sunday afternoon in August when young blood and old feels sand and surf beckoning, away from the hot, crowded city to the vast waters and the cool breezes of Lake Michigan.

"Dad, Tasha and I would like to go to the lake, too. We can meet you at the chapel, spend some time at the beach, and
~~~

then drive back to Grand Rapids. Can I take the car?"

Lisa was sixteen, had just received her driver's license, and had not yet driven the freeways on her own.

"Honey, I'm not comfortable with that; you've never driven there, you may even have a hard time finding it, and the freeways are busy because of the weekend."

"Trust me, Dad. I'm a good driver, I know how to find it, and we'll be careful."

"Oh, Mr. Baron, Lisa is an awesome driver, and I know the way, too. Please, can we go?"

I look at Ruth, but I know she's leaving it up to me.

I swallow hard, and I give in.

It's what parents do, because they love their kids.

And sometimes they don't, and shouldn't, because they love their kids.

~~~

The worship service starts with some singing. My mind is more on the two missing girls than on the songs. Still, when we sing "What a Friend we have in Jesus," the uneasy feeling of something pending, something not good, intensifies. When the minister takes his place in the pulpit, I have already expected the messenger who now makes his way to the podium to whisper something in the minister's ear. And I expect the minister to ask next if there are a Henry and Ruth Baron in the audience. But, when it comes, a piece of cold steel drops around the heart to keep it immobile. We get up and walk to the side door where someone beckons us. Reality has already shifted into another dimension. It's as if we're turning into robots, detaching from the conscious, feeling self. Outside, we see a police car and two officers. That's when blood freezes, before, much later, it cascades through all the veins and arteries into turbulent waves of emotion.

"Do you have a daughter Lisa?"

"Yes."

"She's been in an accident."

All thinking stops as you wait for what comes next.
~~~

~~~

Heading west, the two friends soon leave the humidity of the city behind. Ah, the exhilaration of freedom! The freedom of driving somewhere on the open roads, just the two of them, Lisa and Natasha. Cool breezes and sand between their toes only an hour away. They feel the exuberance of independence, of adventure, and the limitless powers of their youth. They feel hungry for life, for experience, and yes, for food.

After seeing some friends in Zeeland, they stop at a Dairy Queen along the way, near Holland. There they enjoy an early supper, and then take dessert to go. Lisa has a Reese's Pieces Blizzard between her legs and keeps getting spoonfuls while driving. They are listening to a tape of Wally Pleasant, a local humorous musician they like. Life feels free and vital, with windows partway down, music turned up, and the two teens boisterously laughing and singing along with Wally, having the time of their life.

Traffic is busy on US 31, particularly southbound, with many returning from a weekend up north and from a day at nearby beaches. The Mazda 323, on cruise control, hums along smoothly at over 60 mph, though the speed limit on that stretch is 55. Lisa is driving in the northbound left lane. Up ahead she will need to make a left turn toward Lake Michigan and the Conference Grounds.

Getting to the bottom of her Blizzard, Lisa looks down to find a last spoonful. At that moment, the left front wheel edges off the pavement. None of her training and experience has prepared her for this. She looks up when the steering wheel begins to shake and jerks it hard to the right to get back on the road.

Then a scream.

As she loses control and consciousness, the Mazda hits the median, a tire blows, the rear axle breaks, the car flips and slides upside down across the median strip and the southbound lane of traffic, finally coming to a stop, tilted on the driver's side.
~~~

Tasha feels totally disoriented and shaken. She looks at Lisa. Lisa is hanging by her seatbelt. She doesn't move and Tasha thinks Lisa might be dead. There is blood dripping from a cut on her head. Instinct takes over. She knows she has to get Lisa out of the car in case it should explode. She unbuckles her own seatbelt and falls to the roof of the car. She tries to unbuckle her friend, too. It's really hard. And she doesn't think of how it might be bad to move Lisa. She has to get help for her friend. Somehow she manages to crawl out through the backseat window to get help. She sees a lady and a man coming toward her. The lady sits her down on the side of the road. But Tasha has to help Lisa. She tries to get up, but each time she tries, the lady keeps pulling her back, talking to her, trying to calm her. Natasha is shivering violently in the summer heat. Someone brings a blanket, and the lady wraps it around her.

Then the police come. And a fire truck. And an ambulance. Amidst all the noise and commotion, the lady holds Tasha, talking to her, softly, soothingly. Tasha is scared to leave her when she, too, has to enter the ambulance. Before the doors shut behind her, she looks back at the lady with the blond, curly hair. The lady waves. To Natasha, she is an angel.

~~~

You wait for the words you never want to hear: "I'm sorry; your daughter didn't make it."

Instead we hear: "Your daughter was hurt and taken by ambulance to the Grand Haven hospital. Her friend is okay." And instantly the heart lurches into action: alive, yes!! Then moves to concern: but how serious is Lisa?

"Is she hurt badly?"

"We think she'll be all right. She was coming to when the ambulance took her away."

"Thank you."

We go back to tell our friends. They want to come with us to the hospital. We don't talk. Thoughts and emotions
~~~

tumble and churn together: what happened where is she hurt is it her face is she going to be ok oh God please not her brain . . . !!!

In the chapel at the Conference Grounds, the minister tells the audience about the awful day when he lost a teenage child in a fatal car crash. Then he leads in prayer for the parents and their child who was in an accident. Five hundred people praying...

A policeman meets us at the entrance to Emergency. He tells us: "They were going too fast. Other drivers told us that they had the windows rolled down and music turned up high. Not sure whether she was buckled in."

Why is he telling us this now? We want to see Lisa.

We enter Emergency. We see Natasha and hug her. They lead us to a room. We stop at the door. We're not allowed to come in or talk to her, but we can see her. Our hearts fill up. Our eyes do, too. She's alive! Thank God we still have her!

Still, it's a scary sight; her bloody hair caked to her scalp. She's been vomiting, too. And just now, she's having a seizure. They need to take more x-rays.

As she's wheeled out on the stretcher, Lisa sees us. Tears well up in her eyes as she squeezes out the words: "I'm so sorry." We give her a tight smile and tell her it's all right. Oh yes, it's all right!

We wait.

When the doctor comes back, he says that there's some swelling of the brain, a sign of closed-head injury, and that Lisa needs to be taken to Butterworth in Grand Rapids by ambulance.

Our car is still at our friends' cottage, so we take our friends' car and head back to Grand Rapids. We take Tasha with us. We feel so grateful that Tasha's only injury is a sprained finger, but we're tight with worry about Lisa's brain injury. We talk very little.

In Grand Rapids we drop Tasha off at her home, explaining briefly what happened; we feel the need to apologize for our daughter's accident. They understand.

Then we hurry on to the hospital.

~~~

We enter Butterworth Emergency. We're told that Lisa's been admitted to the ICU. A social worker comes to meet us and offers her services. It increases our anxiety: do we really need this?

Finally we're led to Lisa's room. In the shadows we see her form on the bed. There are tubes and monitors, but she's *there* and getting the care she needs. And there's relief in that.

This is not a time to talk. She's heavily medicated and obviously in discomfort. But it's enough now just to touch her, to hold her hand, to kiss her cheek, and to whisper our love.

When we leave, she's alone with her pain, her intense discomfort, her thoughts, and the nightmares to come.

~~~

"what really happened . . . oh . . . yes . . .

"I feel sick and I'm scared . . . how could this happen . . .

"so much noise . . . so much noise . . . are they cutting me out? I'm floating away from my body . . . away . . . away . . . but they're loading me into the ambulance now . . . and somebody is asking me questions . . . my name . . . what year . . . where I'm from . . . but I can't think . . . I can't remember . . . who's president . . . I say Jefferson . . . the man in the ambulance says to just rest in the arms of Jesus . . .

"I feel so guilty . . . I've caused so much trouble . . . I see my parents looking at me . . . tears in their eyes . . . but aren't they angry? . . . thinking that I deserved this . . . for letting them down . . . for making them take time off from work now . . . for wrecking that wonderful car . . . for all those bills they will have to face . . .

"I can hardly move . . . I feel so rotten inside . . . and

I'm so hot . . . will I ever feel better again? . . . will I ever get better again? . . . but I'm still alive . . . thank you, Jesus . . . but why . . . why did God spare my life . . . is there a reason . . . is my life really important?"

~~~

In our waking hours, what is in our mind constantly: how achingly important life is!

I go to look at the Mazda, that pert little beauty we had enjoyed driving so much. There, in the vehicular cemetery, it sags among the casualties of other violent traffic accidents: ripped, torn, smashed, dented, gashed, bloodied, broken – a mute but chilling statement of its last doomed ride. I stare and wonder, awe-filled: why are those girls still alive? Why did they tumble and skid across two lanes of heavy traffic and not get hit? It's a question that stays with you the rest of your life. That, and the vulnerability of life. That, and the preciousness of life.

~~~

We spend many hours in the hospital with Lisa for the next eight days. Doctors tell us that sometimes closed-head injuries cause personality changes. She will probably have memory trouble; learning might be more difficult for a while. We worry about that.

There are days when she is very sick, very sore, and sometimes very feverish from infections.

> "So you lie in bed, feeling the pain. It's getting better but not fast enough. You don't feel like doing anything, definitely don't feel like eating, but you force yourself to. And the doctors tell the nurses to make you walk. So you walk and it's slow and you feel so ugly and afterward you just lie in bed like you were about 100 years old and you wait for the pain to fade.
>
> "The nurses and doctors don't come as often anymore. You've already got bruises and marks and

infection from their IVs and blood samples and you don't like the way they're always asking questions and shining lights in your eyes when you're just so tired. Just let me be. But you act like you feel just a little bit better and they expect you to run a marathon. But at least when you sleep you can't feel the pain.

"It hurts to cry. Your neck aches and your head throbs. Your nose gets all stuffed up and tears run down your face in cold wet rivers. But I cry. I cry alone in the dark. I cry because I'm scared and I don't know the answers. I'm just scared and lonely."

Siblings come to see her, and friends, and our pastor, and her church elder, and many other church members are praying hard for Lisa' full recovery.

"I had over forty visitors and thirteen of these came more than once. They kept my room cheerful with cards and flowers and even teddy bears.

"So many people I didn't even know prayed for me daily. This is not to mention all of my family, friends, teachers and parents' friends who kept me in their prayers. I was so thankful because I felt like people truly cared.

"I never realized how precious and fragile life is. Most people, especially my age, have no idea. They think they are invincible, as I did, driving around with my friends. I'd get rides home with kids from Youth Group and they'd speed along, the music blaring. I thought that was the way you were *supposed* to drive. It didn't seem cool to actually follow all the rules. Rules were made to be broken.

"And I considered myself a good driver, which meant I was a pretty aggressive driver. I'd get mad if someone went under the speed limit. Didn't anyone know that you're supposed to go *above* the speed limit?

"Now I know."

~~~

Lisa's condition gradually improves. Our hope gradually becomes confidence that our youngest will be physically well again. And mentally? Will learning come as easily to her as it always had? We pray that it will, and that we will be patient with the mood changes that will plague her initially.

After eight days at Butterworth, she is transferred to Mary Free Bed for a week of physical therapy. It is a hard week for her. She misses being part of the first weeks of school. She misses the church retreats and the Luis Palau meetings she had prepared for. She misses home. And the therapy is so rigorous, painful, and exhausting. But gradually she begins to walk again; gradually she begins to feel more normal again. She knows that most of the patients there with her will never be able to say that. And she knows that many of them are accident victims, too. Some will never walk again. Some will never hug again. Some will never be able to go to school again. For the first time in her sixteen years she knows, really knows and feels how blessed she is. God has spared her life. But she has learned how vulnerable she is and what a very special gift life really is. Maybe that is the purpose of the accident, she thinks, because that's what she had needed to learn.

~~~

And what do parents learn when one of their children has a brush with death?

These parents learned the force of love so strong that it nearly makes one faint. And the taste of fear so harrowing that it leaves one's heart hollow. But with a constant eye on the flickering light of hope. And with the groaning of prayers, wrestling with God in the night. And when the fear passes, the beam of hope strong again, the prayers heard, the words of Shakespeare teaching them, as never before: "This thou perceivest, which makes thy love more strong, to love that well which thou must leave ere long."

We watch as Lisa lovingly tucks in her sleepy little boy, as she bustles in the kitchen making cookies with her young daughter, as she leads a workshop for mentors of college students. Our hearts fill up. We taste the sweetness of the gift of grace and the overwhelming flush of gratitude that has no words.

The Missing One

by H. J. Baron

Jean heard the car pull up in the driveway. She knew it was David by the rumble of the leaky muffler on his red Monza. She pulled the baking sheet with the last batch of cookies from the oven as her son came rushing through the side door into the kitchen with a cheery "Hi, Mom," then his tall, lanky frame bending down to give his mom a quick kiss. She smelled the cold winter air on him, and his youthful vitality, while he eagerly inhaled the fresh-baked smell of his favorite chocolate chip cookies.

"Wow, Mom, that really smells good!"

"Hello, son, it's good to see you! Are you staying for supper?"

"No, not tonight, Mom, I've got to get to the license office yet, and tonight we're planning on going to the hockey game.

"So why don't I quick make us some tea and then we'll sit down and see how the cookies turned out. How does that sound?"

"Sounds great! I'll look for the stuff I need for my new tab while you make the tea, then."

A few minutes later, mother and son sat by the table over a cup of tea, munching on warm, tasty chocolate chip cookies. They talked about Carol and Ben's anniversary dinner a couple of nights ago at the Down to Earth Restaurant.

"Mom, I'm so glad you invited me, too, 'cause I had a really, really good time!"

"I'm glad you enjoyed it, honey. I think we all did. It was Dad's idea to invite you, you know."

"I want to thank him, too, next time I see him. I had a great time."

And so they talked about ordinary daily life things, which sometimes in retrospect become extraordinary. But on this late Tuesday afternoon in January there was a feeling of something very special about these few minutes together, intimately linked by the love mother and son felt for each other.

David glanced at the kitchen clock, which showed 4:45, and jumped up. "Sorry, Mom, I got to go. The Secretary of State Office closes at five. Thanks for the cookies!" He grabbed the papers off the table and was out the door. Jean watched him go, fold his tall frame into the car, start the engine and back out the driveway. She had turned back to putting the teacups away when she heard the squeal of the brake, heard the door slam, and there was David dashing back into the kitchen. She felt his strong arms around her, his long hair on her cheek as he hugged and kissed her. "I love you, Mom. Bye now." Then he was gone.

Jean looked after her youngest son with wonder and a smile. Something called "mother love" made her heart glow warmly. She turned to clear the table and begin preparations for supper.

But her thoughts stayed on David, the son who often came home to enjoy a good meal, who was always happy, always thoughtful, and whose love for his parents had always been palpable, never giving them a cross word. Not that his life had been particularly easy. School had never come easy to him, though with help from his parents he had made it more or less. But he had never fit easily inside the box. He had such an easygoing, fun-loving nature and hated the drudgery of menial tasks. He needed to be interested to be motivated, and so he had needed going after sometimes. But he had never been resentful or disagreeable. And it was always a joy to have him stop by to enjoy a good meal at home.

Jean was about to open the fridge to take out a head of lettuce, when she paused. She still felt his strong arms around her, his lips on her cheek. Why did it suddenly remind her of last summer when David had left on his long hitchhiking trek? With a quick shake of her head she dismissed the thought, and opened the crisper drawer for the lettuce.

~~~

David knew it was going to be a fine night when he hung up the phone.

"What's up?" asked Dave Berghuis, his close friend, while chomping down on his homemade burrito.

"Hockey game tonight." David smiled back, obviously relishing the prospect.

"Calvin playing?" Dan Brinks, one of Dave's housemates, who had just walked in and overheard, asked the question.

"Yep. You guys want to join us?"

"No can do, I got to work," said Dan.

"And I have to write a paper that's due tomorrow," added Dave. "Who's all going?"

"Dave Lock and Stewart Huizenga are picking me up. Too bad you guys can't make it, it should be a blast."

"If I get my paper done, I'll join you at GREATS afterward," promised Dave.

"Great, dude, I'll see you there then. We've got to give Stewart a good send-off, you know."

"That's right, he's leaving tomorrow, isn't he? I'll be there, then."

"Hey, have a good time, Dave!" Dan took a long look at his friend and saw the pleasure on his face. "I'll see you tomorrow, right?"

"Yeah, see you tomorrow, Dan."
~~~

It had already been a good day for David Tamminga. He'd made it to the Secretary of State Office before it closed. He'd stopped home and seen his mom. His smile grew even bigger as he remembered their little talk and the homemade cookies.

But then he remembered another thing. He'd been ready to drive off when he felt like someone was nudging him into an irresistible impulse to say what his heart was suddenly feeling intensely. He had rushed back to his mom, surprising her with his reappearance.

He wondered even now what had brought that on.

But it had been sweet. The love he had always had for his parents for some reason felt especially strong today. He knew he was blessed to have their love, too, even when he messed up. Even when he lacked some of the self-discipline they valued. Even when he struggled to find his niche. And now, after one semester, he knew he was at the right place, the Kendall School of Design to study furniture design. Life was good.

He looked at his watch – almost 9:30. His ride would be by soon. What better way to end a good day than at a hockey game with buddies!

~~~

The Jolly Roger ice hockey arena was a raucous but merry mixture of the sounds of skates scratching, hockey sticks slapping, partisan fans screaming, referees whistling – everything that makes attending hockey games an addictive kind of pleasure. As occasional hockey players themselves on the Calvin College intramural team, The Cement Heads, the three Calvin team fans really got into the action. The speed, finesse, and aggressive grit of the game never failed to give a high adrenaline thrill not only to the players but, contagiously, also to those who were whooping it up in the stands.

During intermission, Stewart announced to David Tamminga: "You know, I'm thinking of doing something like you did last summer. I really am. You're glad you did it,
~~~

right?"

"Definitely! Hey, that's great, dude! Did you tell your folks yet?"

"No, I'm just starting to think about it. Did you hitchhike all the way?"

"No, Dave Lock wanted to go to Alberta to look for a summer job, so he drove us out from Grand Rapids to Montana in his Datsun and dropped us there in the middle of nowhere. From then on we were on our own. I went with Jeroen Kooi, you know, that dude from the Netherlands who was at Calvin for a year. You're not thinking of doing it solo, are you?"

"I don't know yet. I can just imagine what my mom is going to say about it, you know."

"With me, it was my dad who was against it. He thought I should be making some money for college. But you know, my mom actually encouraged the whole idea. Maybe she thought it might help me find myself, or something."

"Did it? Find yourself, I mean?"

"Hey, it was good, you know. I saw a whole different side of life with all different types of people and all, so yeah, it made me do some thinking."

"So you went way out West, right?"

"Oh yeah: Montana, Wyoming, Colorado, Utah, Arizona, Nevada, California. I fell in love with San Francisco, dude. You haven's seen a city till you've seen Frisco. And those California beaches – really cool, dude. Anyway, then we went up along the coast through Oregon and Washington to Vancouver, B.C. After Jeroen left me in Vancouver to fly back to Holland, I went on by myself to Alberta, where my sister worked in a Provincial Park. From there I took the bus to get back home."

"What did you do to keep yourself alive?"

"We scrounged whenever and wherever we could, you know? I couldn't believe how many kind people there are. All along the way we met people who let us camp in their back yard, fed us, helped us with directions, everything. Sometimes restaurants would let us wash dishes for our meal. That was a really cool part of the whole experience."

Stewart looked thoughtful. "You know, David, I think I need to do that, too, before I settle down in a job or something, you know what I mean? I want to see more of life than what I've seen so far."

"That's how I felt, so go for it, Stu!"

The horn blast signaled the end of intermission. Players were getting back on the ice, fans were returning back to their seats, and the referees were ready to blow the whistle for the beginning of the third period. The guys settled down for the last stretch. Calvin was one goal down. The tension was building.

~~~

"Hello, Jean, I'm home." With that Rev. Louis Tamminga walked into the kitchen, where his wife was busily cutting a salad for supper.

Lou, as he was known by family and friends, was a man of cheerful disposition with a ready laugh, but quick to empathize – an ideal confluence of qualities for a director of Pastor-Church Relations at the denominational headquarters of the Christian Reformed Church in Grand Rapids, Michigan. He dropped his briefcase in his study, then came back to the kitchen.

"Anything I can help you with, dear?" He bent his lean frame over the slow cooker and inhaled the appetizing odors with pleasure.

"No, thanks, go ahead and read the paper; it'll be another ten minutes or so."

"All right. Have you been up to anything special today?"

Dicing some carrots now, Jean answered slowly, with a smile: "Well, yes, I'd say so."

Lou was on the way to his favorite chair in the family room, when he stopped and turned to look at his wife. He'd
~~~

noticed the special tone in her voice, and he saw the special look on her face, like a mother's tone and look when she watches her baby toddler reach for her and she says, "Aw, come to Mommy, sweetie."

"Hmm, what happened?"

"David stopped in, and we had tea and cookies together, and we had a little chat."

"Ah, how nice. How was he?"

"He seems really happy, like he's got it together and knows where he's going."

"Yes, I think he's on the way now. That's a good feeling, isn't it?"

Jean mixed the carrot pieces in with the salad now, then stopped and looked up at her husband. "And you know what made it really special?"

"No, what?"

Lou gave her his full attention now.

"I had heard David start the car, and I thought he had already left, when all of a sudden he was back, ran up to me, gave me a big bear hug and kiss, and told me he loved me. Now what can be more special than that!"

Lou walked back to Jean, and said: "I know, not even this," as he, too, embraced his wife and kissed her.

She reveled in the moment. "Hey, dear; you know your hugs are special, too. I feel so blessed today. It almost makes me feel a little afraid."

Lou laughed. "Oh come now, why?"

"I don't know."

~~~

GREATS was a late-hour restaurant-bar, and the hangout of choice for the post-hockey game crowd, particularly for the Canadian student contingent of the Calvin College hockey game fans, including some of the players. The place had great burritos, the beer flowed freely, the atmosphere high octane. And for Stewart Huizenga it was a special night of spending their last party together, a kind of farewell cele-
~~~

bration, for he was dropping out of Calvin to return home to Wisconsin the next day; his parents needed him.

And so the Calvin crowd partied. It was a tight group that knew each other, enjoyed each other, and were always eager to blow off all the tensions of the day and the game.

"Hey, everybody, I want you to see how David opens a can of beer," shouted Dave Berghuis to the gang. "Will somebody go get him a can over here?"

Stewart was soon back with a can of Coors. "Here, my treat, ole' buddy."

David Tamminga stood up, dramatically spread his arms, beer can in one hand, to draw them all around him, and while Dave Berghuis hushed the gathering group, with a mock-serious expression on his handsome face, David placed the can tight against his right eye. Slowly he began to turn the can, as if unscrewing the top, while stealthily making the pressure-releasing fizzing sound that gradually increased in volume as he kept rotating the Coors against his eye. For a moment the guys were mesmerized and totally fooled, then hooted and hollered as David plunked the can down on the table and asked for another kind of can opener.

"That's the last one you're going to pull on me, buddy," laughed Stewart, giving David a friendly poke in the ribs.

No doubt the exuberance of youth was intoxicating that night.

And the beer flowed freely.

When at last, well past 1:00 a.m. now, the last of the revelers headed for their cars, Stewart Huizenga put his arm around David Tamminga's neck and said: "Hey Dave, I'm gonna miss you guys, you know that?"

David, taking the last puff on his Winston, inhaled deeply, then, serious for a moment, stopped, blew the smoke out, flicked the butt away, grabbed his friend to give him a spontaneous hug, and said: "We're gonna miss you, too, dude. I hope you get a chance to come back and look us up. I want to know all about that trip you're gonna take, you know?"

Then the two slid into the front seat with Dave Lock in the Lock family's Buick station wagon, the three of them hunkered close together for the short ride home.

No big deal, of course, for buddies to say goodbye.

But sometimes it is.

It was a cold winter night, but the party spirit still lingered, and the high feeling of youthful vitality that gives the illusion of invincibility.

But they weren't.

Invincible, that is.

Dave Lock found himself behind Jack De Gelder's little Honda Civic, heading north on the East Beltline at about 40 mph. Too slow for Dave. He would show them the power of an 8-cylinder Buick engine. He gunned it, the engine roared, the big car leaped ahead, soon hit 60 mph, whipped around Jack's car, cut back right in front of him, failed to cut back into the lane, left the road, went airborne, flipped as it disappeared into the deep gully, doors flying open, bodies ejecting, finally coming to rest against the culvert.

Then all was dark. Pitch dark. And silent.

~~~

It's Wednesday, January 19, 1983, early, before there's a glimmer of a sunrise.

A doorbell rings. And again. And again.

Rev. Louis Tamminga gropes for the alarm clock now, but can't see the dial. When the doorbell rings again, he's instantly awake, feeling a stab of fear hitting the pit of his stomach. He stumbles to the living room, draws the curtain aside, and peers into the night.

He sees a police car at the curb under the street light, then an officer's uniform by the door; other figures, too. The fear grows inside like a cold fire.

There are strange shadows in the living room, cowering, as if they know what's yet unspoken.
~~~

Through the small window in the door now, he sees the three silent figures, the embodiment of the eerie shadows inside.

He turns on the light, tries to open the front door, but it sticks, as if reluctant to allow the tidings to enter the house. When it opens, all three heads turn at the same time.

Two officers and Rev. Bernie Pekelder (Pek), former chaplain and now the college's vice president for student affairs, enter.

"Bernie, seeing you here at this hour bodes no good," Lou begins, and there's a tremble in his voice."

"No, it's not good," Pek responds softly and gently.

"David?"

Pek nods. "David died in an accident, Louis."

Jean is still in the bedroom, eyes fixed straight ahead, filled with hollow fear. "He's been in an accident," she thinks, "and they're going to take him home pretty soon. I have to get ready to take care of him."

She hears the name David as she enters the living room. She sucks in her breath, is momentarily rooted in place. Lou leads her gently to the sofa, where they sit down.

Then he tells her softly: "David has gone to be with the Lord."

Jean reaches for Lou's hand. They squeeze tight. And with those words and that touch they feel an infusion of power enter their soul and the arms of God gently enfolding them.

Pekelder and the officers look with amazement and relief at their composure.

Then in short, sober sentences the officers relate the facts of the accident that has claimed the lives of three promising young men.

The parents look at each other, their souls struggling to escape the grip of an intractable reality: David, tall, wonderful David with his wide-set eyes, his broad, engaging grin . . .

An overwhelming vision comes upon Jean: "I see him clearly," she says. "He is among a great multitude of people walking up to God."

It's a sustaining vision for this moment, and for long thereafter.

There's silence.

Then, "Are you prepared to identify the body?" one of officers asks.

Lou nods.

"Why don't you come with us; we'll drive you," offers the other officer.

"Oh, thank you, but I think we prefer to drive ourselves," responds Lou. "We'll follow you, if that's all right."

~~~

Jack De Gelder watches in horror as the Buick leaves the roadway, hits the gully, flips, and disappears.

He pulls off. There's only one thought in his mind: get help!

He runs back to GREATS, almost a mile away.

Meanwhile, more cars with Calvin students pull up behind.

They rush down into the gully in stunned disbelief.

The Buick, upside down, is resting at an angle against the culvert.

They see David Tamminga's body pinned partly underneath.

Five or six young men try to lift the tilted car off the body.

Among them is Nelson Greidanus, David's best friend and neighbor in early grade school years.

He and others grab the heavy car and tip it enough for Colin Ward to pull David from underneath.

In the cold night steam rises from David's still warm body.

Colin cradles David in his arms.

He is still alive, but gasping and choking.

Then Colin feels his friend's body go limp.

The others gather around, silent witnesses to the un-
~~~

speakable – Death.

Three friends, vibrantly alive among them just minutes ago, now sprawled motionless, lifeless, on the frozen ground before them.

In the distance they hear the first sound of sirens.

~~~

On that cold, clear night, now edging toward morning, the two parents drive slowly toward a reality still beyond comprehension.

They pray as they ride through the strange, forsaken city streets, the rear lights of the police cruiser ahead.

"Oh Lord, be with us now. Oh Lord, give us the strength we need for this. Oh Lord . . . "

They're grasping for comfort. They tell each other: "He's now meeting Opa Hagen, and the apostle Paul, and Christ himself . . . "

Now the hospital is in sight. The cruiser swings into the Emergency driveway entrance. They park behind the police car.

Then they go in. Bernie Pekelder, too.

They are ushered into the elevator. They descend to the basement, to the place of the dead.

They clasp each other's hand again as they enter the morgue.

They see the three bodies: Dave Lock, Stewart Huizenga, and yes, *their* David.

"Our David. Oh Lord, *our* David." It's a whisper, but the force of it tears at their insides.

They approach the body more closely now.

It's as if their son is deeply engaged in something, fully concentrating on what demands his attention, his eyes closed, his face peaceful, though scratched.

He's still wearing his new jacket he was so proud of.

His neck looks swollen, but there's no sign of blood.

They touch his hair, as they had so often done, that thick, curly hair, always too much of it, but so beautiful.
~~~

"This is not our David," they say to each other, as they need to. "Our David has gone to the redeemed with Christ."

They hang on to that thought with all the fibers of their faith as they leave the morgue.

Then they enter a small prayer room, all five of them.

Pekelder prays with them, pleading with God for strength and the Spirit's comfort.

Still almost preternaturally composed, Lou prays, too: "Dear Father, we commend the son we love so much to your eternal love and keeping. Oh Lord, have mercy!"

Then Jean prays, for the other parents who have not yet been notified.

There is silence in the room, the silence of feelings and forces that have no words.

On the drive home, the parents are amazed at their own clarity of thought. It's as if their minds have been cleared of everything except to focus on this single event that has not yet become wholly real to them. And they feel God's presence very near.

At home, in the kitchen, they pray again.

Jean pours water to make tea.

Very little is said.

They decide to go back to bed, not to sleep, but to plan what now has to be done.

They reach for the Bible, find a card with a passage that comforts them.

They talk about calls that need to be made.

They pray again.

Then they weep in each other's arms, clinging to each other, the pain beginning to pour out: "Oh Lord, our boy, our son, our David, his face, his smile, his eyes, his big strong hands, his hug . . . "

And they comfort each other: he's not far, he's with Jesus, he's in great joy . . .

When they get up, they call their children.

Jean reads the number, Lou dials.

Ben first, to catch him before he leaves for work.

Then Tim, then Mark, then Ken and Nancy, then Karen.

Before each call they pray. After each call they give thanks for thc courageous response of each child.

And then other calls to friends, to family in the Netherlands, to the people in the office, in the church.

~~~

The next few days are a whirl of calls and visitors and decisions and tears.

The parents, the siblings, the large circle of David's friends – everyone struggles to come to terms with this numbing reality: three strong young men struck down at the beginning of their adult lives, three sons full of dreams and anticipation shared by their parents.

But there is comfort in the visits and embraces of others who care deeply. Through them they feel the closeness of God.

And through it all, David emerges almost more real than he had been in real life. Their minds and hearts are filled with what David had meant to them. They struggle to accept that he is not here anymore and never would be again.

The Tamminga family gathers, parents and children and spouses, as they had only a month earlier, around the Christmas tree, in a spirit of celebration.

They talk about that time, now in a spirit of deep sorrow.

After Christmas, David had asked all to come to his place for a meal.

David had been the only one at his house. Todd Cooper and Paul Faber, his housemates, had gone home for Christmas. And that had made it all the more special for the family.

Their son had prepared a splendid meal.

It became an unforgettably fine evening.

They remember.
~~~

They receive it now as God's farewell gift, in tears.

Dad and Mom tell them how only a few days ago, on Carol and Ben's wedding anniversary, David had joined them all for dinner at the Down to Earth Restaurant, and what a wonderfully sweet time they had enjoyed together.

Three days later, the accident.

Still incomprehensible to all of them.

Dad tells them of his long stay in Africa during November and most of December. Mom had been with Oma, her sick mother in Ontario, much of the time.

"David was there all by himself in Grand Rapids," says Dad. "He was on my mind a lot. I sometimes saw his face – the expressions when he would make his little observations. I felt so much love for him. And I prayed for him a lot. I prayed that he would be all right."

They nod.

They hold each other.

They cry.

~~~

Hundreds come to the De Vries Funeral Home to meet the family.

They cannot view the body; the casket is closed.

The family is overwhelmed by the large number of students who count themselves as David's friends. They speak so fondly of his friendship, his upbeat nature, his family stories, his humor, his love of rock, his creativity, his thoughtfulness, his special ability to listen to their confidences.

David Berghuis, a special friend, says tearfully: "I lost a very dear, very close bosom buddy."

David's pastor, Rev. Gordon Negen of Eastern Avenue Christian Reformed Church, tells the parents of the last Sunday night, when after the service, David had walked up to his pastor to shake hands and thank him for the service.

The family feels blessed amidst their grief.

Eastern Avenue Church is packed for the memorial
~~~

service.

The music, the sermon, the handshakes and hugs and tears of so many provoke feelings that are too deep for words.

The faith profession from the **Messiah,** "I know that my Redeemer liveth," settles deeply inside the soul.

And the violin solo of "When Peace Like a River" imparts a feeling of profound emotion and comfort.

It is as if here the family and the whole church community are giving David back to God.

They leave with the blessing of the beginning of healing.

At the gravesite in Woodlawn Cemetery, brother Mark speaks of the real hope that is theirs.

And sister Karen will long remember the freshly disturbed rich earth, so beautiful in color and texture, the brown oak leaves blowing around, and the dearness of the brother in the grave who in her heart will always remain close.

In the days after the funeral, hundreds and hundreds of cards and letters pour in.

"He was a true gentleman," writes one. Another: "I'll always remember him with the face like an angel's."

Robin Jensen, the chair of Calvin's Art Department writes: "We remember David as a student and friend excited by the potential of creative art in his life."

And from the Kendall School of Design: "David was a fine young man and extremely talented."

But David is no more among them.

The process of grieving really begins when each returns to one's normal routines of life, which suddenly are not normal anymore.

And each one's way of grieving is unique, and needs to be respected.

They talk about that as a family, before they all go their own way again.

The need to freely talk about David, the brother they had loved so much, about his life, his person, his weaknesses and strengths.

The need to face up to the pain of grief, to let it come, yet not to surrender to it and not indulge in it, but to embrace life with more fondness and passion than before.

The need to support each other, and remind each other of their true comfort, of the words from Isaiah that will be on his gravestone: "For I have redeemed you. I have called you by name. You are mine."

But also to realize that though grieving has a beginning, and though it goes through stages, it has no ending.

For the one who has left does not return.

~~~

The children leave.

The parents are alone again.

But there's an aged mother very sick in Ontario.

Jean needs to visit her.

While there, Lou is asked if he can preach for the church in Whitby.

Somehow he consents, and preaches on "My grace is sufficient for you."

The Lord's grace tangibly enables him, less than two weeks after David's death, to bring the passage from 2 Corinthians 12 to bear on the raw wounds of their torn hearts.

Sometime later the two are able to spend four days in a cottage on Lake Michigan, kindly provided by friends.

They've gathered all the pictures and files of mementos of David.

At the cottage they will make an album.

They look at the pictures, from childhood on.

And the notes.

As a very young Sunday school pupil, David wrote: "Oh Dear God may We have lots of fun at church Lord. and may we not get sike of it Lord. And forgive my sins! Amen"

As a boy of almost seven, when he had improved his spelling skills a little, he wrote a school letter: "Dear Mother, Sunday is Mother's Day and I want to tell you that I love you.
~~~

I think you are the best mother in the world. You always make my dinner and you make my supper."

As an eight-year old he wrote a heart-shaped note: "Dear Opa and Oma, I love you very!!very!!very!! much. love and cheers from David"

And there's a note from a sixth grade teacher: "David is a cheerful, friendly pupil who brightens our days . . . !"

There are the drawings of a budding artist at age fourteen.

And there's the pleading note of a seventeen-year old who needs the family car for an important date: "Mom, Dad, Some serious worrying came up to-night about not being able to get the car tomorrow night. You see all the arrangements are set. PLEASE can I have it it is is life or death. Thanks. Love, David"

The parents look at these reminders in a way they never had before.

They see the life that had been their son's, their youngest little boy, such a bundle of creative energy who grew into a beautiful young man with long wavy hair cascading down his head, a ready smile, and gentle eyes with an innocent, open look.

And they feel as never before the intensity of the love they had and have for him.

Often they lose themselves in memories.

They smile. They talk. And they weep.

The healing continues.

But it is not unbroken.

In a letter to his children, Lou writes: "There are moments when the closeness as I experienced it with David becomes almost too much to bear, when I gasp for air, as it were.

But then the Lord lifts me up, and I feel strong again."

But weak, too, sometimes.

For sometimes questions push to the front that can torment:

Why do these terrible things happen?

Why, why, why is a life snuffed out, a strong neck broken by a seemingly random series of uncontrollable events?

Was it God's will that David should die so young, so violently?

Isn't He a God of love?

Could He not have prevented it?

And memories sometimes lead to the pain of regrets.

They search their soul. Had they been good parents?

Yes, David had told others that his parents were the best.

Still, there are the poignant memories of encounters with David that they think now should have been handled with more grace, more understanding; and there were opportunities passed by.

But in time they learn to set boundaries to their questions, to open their hearts to God's love and peace.

They learn to ask God to forgive their shortcomings and inject his healing into the closed chapters of their lives.

And they experience the truth of Psalm 77:9: "No, God had not forgotten to be merciful."

They are able to pick up the threads of life again, sometimes even to enjoy and appreciate the fun of life.

Still, though there is the occasional glow on life's path, there's always a shadow, too.

There come the unpredictable, searing moments of missing David intensely, of a deep sadness creeping over their hearts for the son who is not there.

It can happen when they're working in the garden, with a sudden memory of him coming toward them with his big steps, grin on his face, twinkle in his eyes, grabbing the spade, digging in with that awesome power he had, putting the spade down, picking up his dad as if he were a child, running around the whole back yard with him in his strong arms, and heading for the family room to put him down in his chair, and join his parents for coffee.

But there's goodness in those memories, too, for they affirm the life and the love with which David enriched their lives for his twenty-one years.

~~~

Years later.

The Tamminga family gathers by a tree on the Calvin College campus.

It's a Redbud Crabapple tree.

In springtime it flowers into a lavish feast of fragrant soft pink.

But it's fall now.

Instead of flowers there are small, shiny, bright orange-red fruits.

Some are strewn on the ground below.

Father Tamminga bends down, begins to gently wipe away the tiny apples, the leaves, and the grass clippings that partly cover a square stone with a copper plaque beneath the tree.

The family stands closer to read:

IN MEMORY OF
STEWART L. HUIZENGA
DAVID LOCK
DAVID L. TAMMINGA
JANUARY 19, 1983

As a student body initiative, the tree was planted in the fall of 1983.

Students and faculty raised the needed funds.

Most crab apple trees have four or more major branches.

Ken discovers that this memorial tree had one carefully removed.

Three main branches remain.

One for each of the students.
~~~

Parents and children look at the names.
Beyond the name, they see the face of David.
The memories float back.
And the pain is still there.
The pain of the missing one.

Acknowledgment

The Tammingas kindly supplied me with pictures, mementos, journals, clippings, articles, and reflections related to the tragic event of January 19, 1983. In many instances, the words in this story were taken verbatim from the writings of Rev. Louis Tamminga. I am grateful for their constant readiness to assist.

Others who proved helpful in reconstructing the events of that night and offering insight into the person of David Tamminga include David Berghuis, Jack De Gelder, Nelson Greidanus, and Jeroen Kooi. To all of them my sincere thanks.

The Hand of God

by H. J. Baron

It wasn't a good life in bomb-ravaged Vietnam after the war.

For one thing, the regime set out to purge the country from all its enemies.

That meant that everyone felt spied upon.

And all adults had to attend communist party sponsored "study sessions."

Thousands were sent to "re-education camps" where they were virtual prisoners and doomed to hard labor, sometimes for years.

Besides, unemployment was high. Inflation soared. Food was scarce, and very expensive. More than half of a worker's monthly income was spent on food. Rationing had to be reinstated in 1986 for such essential goods as rice, meat, sugar, and kerosene.

It was a life of abject austerity, if not poverty.

No wonder that millions tried to flee the country, mostly in crudely built or old, dilapidated fishing boats. Fishing boat owners were eager to supplement their meager income by selling space on their boat to people seeking escape. They might also arrange for guides to lead the escapees from their home to the point of departure, typically near a rather remote, southern fishing area. Some of the fishermen in the coastal regions were building boats and charging outrageous amounts of money to get people out of the country. But many of these vessels were deathtraps, and the journey extremely perilous.

And there seemed to be no future for the young, especially not for those whose parents had been working with the American allies in the bloody, intractable war. They were tagged as "children of the enemy."

No wonder, then, that parents dearly wanted a better life for their children and that many sent them on a perilous journey of escape toward the promise of a future.

Escaping the country was, of course, illegal. If caught, one would surely end up in jail. However, a far worse fate awaited many who did escape but never made it to the Promised Land.

This is the story of a teenage girl who risked everything.

~~~

It was May 8, 1986. My-Uyen (pronounced Me Win) was on her way home from school. She knew she was fortunate. Many young people her age, if they were lucky enough to get a job, were working at some menial job with no chance for a high school education. It was only because of her mother's needed skills as an accountant that the government granted her this privilege. She also knew that she would not be allowed to go on to college.

Her mother greeted her at the door, her face serious. "My, you're leaving tomorrow morning. It's all arranged. Now we have much to do to get ready." She drew her seventeen year-old daughter inside.

My-Uyen was stunned, though she had known that this day would come, for it had often been discussed.

"Do I really have to go, Mom?"

There was a note of panic in her voice; she felt her heart race and her hands become shaky.
~~~

"Yes, dear, and you know why."

She looked into her mother's eyes. What she saw there was love, fear, and determination. And yes, she knew the reasons. Her father had explained more than once why he was identified as an enemy of the country. He had worked for the U.S. Army during the war years, in charge of transporting supplies from the military ships to distribution centers. As a daughter of the "enemy," My-Uyen would be barred from pursuing higher education or a profession. It would only be in the United States that she would have an opportunity to achieve her potential.

In the hours that remained, the family drew close together. It became an intimate time of deep feelings and heartfelt words. The knowledge of danger ahead was rooted deep in their bones.

My-Uyen could be caught.

She could drown.

She could fall into wrong hands.

The parting could be final.

Yet, though feeling the dread of each possible scenario chilling their hearts, she would go. For the sake of her future, the parents would pay the clandestine escape organization $1,000 in gold bars, embrace their daughter the next morning in tears, kiss her one more time, and let her go.

That evening, before they said their "good-nights," the mother said softly: "My daughter, I want you to have this. Carry it with you wherever you go, and don't forget me."

Then she placed her own gold ring gently into My-Uyen's hand.

My-Uyen accepted it hesitantly and felt a strong surge of emotion as she folded her hand around it.

She hugged her mother tightly and wordlessly, then hurried out of the room to hide her tears and to sew this precious treasure inside the waistband of the pants she would be wearing in the days ahead.

~~~
~~~

It was May 9, 1986, eight o'clock in the morning.

With a lady from the organization, My-Uyen boarded a bus that would take her many hours south from Saigon to Can Tho.

There a lady guide met her and led her to the city market. In the crowded marketplace, she was placed in the charge of another stranger, though the two were never to be seen together.

Dressed intentionally as a peasant, she was not to attract attention to herself. Staying at some distance from each other, they slowly made their way to the ferry dock.

After crossing the Mekong River, they boarded another bus that took them to Soc Trang. My-Uyen was careful never to give a sign that indicated she was following someone. Sometimes by river taxi, sometimes by van, they finally reached Vinh Chau, near the end of the river that empties into the South China Sea.

It was nearly dark now.

They needed to walk across a muddy rice field to get to the small craft that would take them to the "big fish," the larger boat that was supposed to be ocean-worthy.

Other "boat people" joined them.

They huddled together in the small outboard for what seemed like hours.

Then the leader told them to get ready; they were getting close.

~~~

In the blackness of the night, they began to see the dim outline of a bigger boat, the boat that was waiting for them, and they could hear its engine now.

Soon they pulled alongside.

They would have to make the transfer quickly, before the river police could be alerted and catch them in the act. That would mean prison for sure, if not worse.

People stood up and began to rush to the side.

It was each for him- and herself now.
~~~

Frantically, they began to push and shove to be the first to get on the escape boat.

There were other boats, too, arriving from all directions, whose passengers were all trying to jump onto the "big fish" at the same time.

People were screaming and fighting, afraid of being left behind.

My-Uyen got up, too, but she couldn't get to the rail through all the people fighting for first place.

She went toward the back of the boat, by the outboard engines, where there were fewer jostling for position.

There she figured she would have a better chance to jump onto the other boat.

Her heart was racing now, her nerves taut.

She clutched the small bag with a change of clothes and some provisions tightly to her as she leaped toward freedom.

But in the darkness she missed her step.

To her horror, she felt herself falling toward the engines below, still churning in the water.

She knew then that she was falling toward a certain death.

This would be the end.

Her young life flashed before her.

She thought of her parents, and a great sadness descended on her heart.

Then the inexplicable happened.

Out of nowhere in the darkness, an unseen hand grabbed her, lifted her, and hoisted her into the bigger boat.

She was stunned.

Where did that hand come from?

Whose hand was it?

She never saw a person; she only felt the hand that caught her and would not let her go.

She had no time to cry then; that would come later.

But for now, all she could think of was her moment-by-moment survival.

She was squished among a mass of people in the bottom of the "big fish." The old fishing boat was no bigger than 50 x 6 feet and never intended for crossing the high seas. Many, if not most, of these ill-equipped boats sailed toward the horizon and disappeared without a trace, the victims of poor weather, pirates, or starvation.

But here they were now, a hundred desperate bodies packed into its dark and dank hold like sardines in a can, tensely waiting for another boat to arrive with water and supplies for the journey.

But nobody came. The supply boat must have gotten lost.

And it wasn't safe to wait any longer.

~~~

Thus the boat and its human cargo headed out to sea.

Alarmed voices sounded out: "But we have no food or water! How will we survive? There are babies here that need to be fed!"

But there was no time to worry about that then. They were still close to the land, still likely to be spotted and stopped by the communist patrols.

And if they were, harsh punishment would follow.

They were known to sometimes torture and beat the escapees to death.

Besides, as they were speeding out to where the calmer shore waters give way to the mighty waters of the South China Sea, the ride suddenly became very rough.

The boat was wildly tipping, swinging, rocking in the huge waves, seemingly in danger of capsizing.

People were screaming and throwing up over themselves, while babies screeched in a cacophonous chorus at the boat's violent tossing. One voice yelled out: "Throw that baby out!" Other voices began to join in: "Yes, throw those screaming babies out! We can't stand all that racket!"

The babies' cries had frayed My-Uyen's nerves to a
~~~

thread, too, but now she stared in disbelief at those who were yelling and cursing at the helpless parents to throw their babies out.

"What kind of people are these?" she thought. "How can they, desperately trying to save their own lives, demand the death of these innocent babies? Are these my people?"

She felt shame and disgust. And she cried.

But the wild ride continued.

My-Uyen was sitting next to an oil drum that began to tip and spill some of its contents. Soon the sickening and penetrating stink of fuel oil on her and around her began to mix with the human smells, saturating the unventilated hold.

Again she felt the fear of death and a surging panic squeezing the air from her lungs.

She wanted to hug her parents one more time, to hold on to them for the dear life that was again in jeopardy.

But she had to keep quiet, to hold on to hope.

Someone from the deck cabin came down and called out: "Is there someone here by the name of My-Uyen?"

Puzzled and frightened, she didn't stir at first.

But again the man's voice cut through the total darkness of the hold: "I want My-Uyen to follow me to the deck."

She hesitantly rose, her heart pounding, not knowing what was in store for her. She followed the man up.

When they reached the deck, the man explained: "The captain wants to see you."

She followed the man into the cabin and faced the captain.

"My-Uyen," the captain said, "I know your parents. And I promised your dad that I would try to keep an eye on you. That's why I want you to join us in the cabin. We'll keep you busy. There's plenty to do."

Her heart's pounding calmed. She felt immensely relieved and supremely privileged. For she could now stay on deck, breathe fresh air, away from the horrible stink down in the airless hold where human misery was nearly unbearable.

No one slept much that first scary, stormy night. Many below deck were sick and felt weak.

But when at last the waters calmed somewhat, and dawn ushered in a new day, relief was visible.

They were now on the open sea.

There was no turning back.

My-Uyen stepped outside the cabin and walked to the railing.

She looked up at the infinity of sky and space.

She looked down on the watery depth below.

For the first time in her life, she felt the fear of insignificance.

She was but a tiny dot caught between the immensity of space above and the indifference of a vast ocean below.

There was no escape here.

Should she die here now, no one would know the difference.

She shuddered at the thought.

"I'm too young," she remonstrated. "My life hasn't meant anything yet."

"What then *was* the meaning of life?"

It was a question that would linger.

But now, the fear of the unknown dominated everyone's mind.

When shortly after dawn they were spotted by a Vietnamese patrol boat, tension ran high again.

They knew then that at no time would they be out of danger.

My-Uyen felt the full weight of that, and fear rose again like an acid force within her. But the captain altered his course, so that they were now running parallel with the pursuing patrol boat.

Soon the patrol boat police recognized that the distance between them was too great to catch the escape boat before it would be in international waters.

They turned back, and once again there was a huge

sigh of relief.

But there was no food and no water.

Many already suffered from dehydration, exacerbated by the vomiting. It would only get worse as the temperature rose.

Occasionally a fish would land on deck; it was then quickly grabbed and eaten.

But the whining of children for food and drink was constant.

Some parents had taken a bit of food along and tried to satisfy their children, but most could only sit by helplessly.

When she was asked to join the crew in the cabin again, she was thankful for the distraction.

The captain said: "My-Uyen, we need an extra pair of eyes. We need to scan the horizon in all directions constantly for little dots, which are likely to turn out to be Thai pirates on fishing boats. I want you to stand there," pointing to the right corner of the cabin. "You have responsibility for that part of the horizon. I hope you have good eyes. If you think you see something, holler."

My-Uyen was happy with the responsibility. During the night, too, she would take a shift to monitor the right compass heading. The small bulb illuminating the compass had to be all but covered at night, for they had to observe strictly blackout conditions to remain safe. The crew used a small Vietnamese cap to cover the light. Only a tiny hole was left for My-Uyen to peer through.

The next day she was the first to notice a small dot on the horizon.

She alerted the captain.

The captain stared at the dot, then turned to My-Uyen, and announced simply, "That's a Thai pirate boat coming our way."

She had seen fear in the captain's eyes.

Her mind momentarily went blank at the thought of what she had dreaded most.

She began to shake as she watched the dot gradually grow larger.

Suddenly a voice on deck cried out: "I see a boat coming!"

Tired as they were, the people rushed to see the approaching ship.

But the curt command from the captain interrupted their curiosity:

"It's a pirate ship. All the women and children go below immediately and keep absolutely quiet!"

My-Uyen's blood froze at the thought of what might be coming.

She had heard the ghastly stories of pirate atrocities.

She knew that there was a better than even chance that they would be attacked by Thai fishermen-turned pirates.

She knew that many thousands of refugees like herself had been massacred by these thugs preying on the high seas. They would take whatever gold and hard currency the boat people carried with them, often club and knife the men and dump them into the sea, along with the babies, savagely rape and brutalize the women, especially teenage women, then take the most attractive ones with them to sell to village brothels.

The horrific, heart-stopping stories of survivors had come back to haunt the families left behind in Vietnam.

Knowing what could happen, My-Uyen did not go down as the captain had commanded. She moved to the back of the boat, among the men, and began to smear her face and neck with engine oil.

But she knew that even a repulsive appearance and smell might not save her.

Yet she resolved that she would not be taken. If necessary, she would jump overboard to escape a worse fate than death.

She prayed, as a Buddhist, that her death might be peaceful.

The ship had come close now.

She saw three men on its deck, swarthy pirates wearing sarongs and headbands, but no shirts.

They looked fierce and threatening, hungry for prey.

Another flash of imminent death sliced through her brain.

But once again, the inexplicable happened.

No words were exchanged between the two vessels.

Only some gestures.

Then the pirate ship began to turn away.

My-Uyen did not understand; nobody did.

She thought of the mysterious hand that had saved her. And she received it as another gift.

They were saved!

The relief felt by everyone was deep and intense.

Soon, though, it gave way to a preoccupation with their misery. Emotional and physical exhaustion, hunger, and thirst were taking their toll.

In the cabin, My-Uyen shared with the two captains the little amount of dry rice and dried fruit her mother had given her to take along.

Later that day they met another boat crowded with refugees. The boat was frightfully small, not much larger than a good-sized rowboat, bobbing on the vast ocean waves.

The motley group on the "big fish" looked down on their fellow freedom seekers with pity and wished them good luck.

That night, My-Uyen was shown how to steer the boat by the stars. She didn't know much about stars, but the captain showed her which one to keep the bow of the boat aligned with. It took all her concentration, but it made her feel useful and responsible.

She looked up at the moon hanging high in the night sky over the Pacific; to her it looked like a golden face of hope, and her spirits lifted.

Rain came on the third day as heaven's blessing. Everybody tried to catch the much needed water in bags and whatever containers they could find. They drank what they needed and stored the rest in empty oil drums, not even worrying about the residue of oil in it.

But if their thirst was lessened, their hunger was not.

The men in the cabin were weakening, too, and that worried My-Uyen. She knew that they needed all the strength they could muster. The fate of a hundred people depended on it. And she had no more food of her own to share.

So she decided to see what she could scrounge up among her fellow travelers for the well-being of the crew.

To her dismay, no one offered anything, except some cigarettes.

But even those were gladly accepted by the captains and helped to keep them going.

~~~

When at last the Malaysian coast came into view, excitement rose high.

My-Uyen watched closely as they neared the shore. It looked like they were landing near a tourist resort.

Were those people waving at them?

Would they actually be welcomed here?

Would this be the beginning of freedom?

She couldn't wait.

Now they noticed a border patrol boat approaching them.

Apparently the exhausted boat people made an impression, for the patrol boat turned toward the beach, docked, and soon came back with gifts gathered from the beach's sunbathers.

Some had food to give for the hungry boat people. Others gave toys for the children. Adults and children greedily accepted the proffered gifts and were basking in their sudden good change of fortune.

But it was short-lived.

Soon they followed the patrol boat to a nearby harbor
~~~

where they docked and disembarked.

Once on shore, they looked back in utter disbelief that this flimsy, weather-beaten and broken-down vessel had safely carried them over the ocean waters!

Suddenly the police were there. And they were not there to bring gifts.

A scrawny, sullen-looking policeman barked the order: "Attention! Everyone of you is to turn in all the disposables you have on you. That includes all food and cigarettes! Put everything in the big container right here. And do it now!"

The little fellow tried to puff himself up to look as fierce and threatening as possible, but some people were so outraged, they turned their backs on him and threw their stuff away instead, especially whatever food and cigarettes they had hoarded.

My-Uyen watched in disbelief when she saw the food people still had on them, the food they had refused to share with the crew when she had begged for it.

Again, it made her angry and ashamed of her fellow refugees.

After torching the boat that had somehow navigated the treacherous miles from South Vietnam to Malaysia, the Malaysian police escorted the refugees to a temporary holding camp.

But were they safe now?

My-Uyen shook her head as if to shake off the demons of terror that lingered, but she couldn't as they entered the camp.

This is where their refugee life would begin.

And it began in horror.

The same wiry little policeman was pumping himself up again as he climbed a platform to issue the next command in a voice that grated like sandpaper over an open wound: "I want all the women and children to move to the left side, and I want you to do it NOW! ALL WOMEN AND CHILDREN MOVE AWAY FROM THE MEN NOW!"

His cohorts hustled around, busily pushing women and children away from the men and toward another nearby building.

There the women were told to take off their clothes.

They had no choice but to oblige, eagerly assisted by the unscrupulous Malaysian police who debased their helpless victims by groping and fondling, and looking for any jewelry or gold they might've been trying to hide.

Then the women were sent to the showers.

Later, to the helpless victims' horror, police selected their rape victims.

But My-Uyen again was saved, this time from sexual assault and humiliation. She had started menstruating just hours before, and that made her an untouchable to the men. They did not lay a finger on her.

Much later, when she replayed these series of frightening and degrading events in her mind, the wonder and the gratitude would begin to grow in her.

They were there for two days, then sent on to another transition camp, Parang.

Here they could sleep on cots and eat coconuts.

But this camp, too, did not turn out to be a safe place.

For there was a roving, omnipresent Papa, a tall, slender, hirsute Malaysian, dressed in typical communist green garb, with an inexhaustible appetite for women. He had announced at their coming, when he introduced himself with a creepy smile: "I'm here to welcome your stay. Call me Papa, and Papa likes women."

This predator would cozy up to them, pretend to be their protector, accompany them to the bathroom, and find a way to assault them.

My-Uyen feared this "dirty old man" intensely.

Once more a benefactor saved her.

One of the captains from the "Big Fish" took her under his wing, like a brother, and told Papa that the young lady was his wife.

Papa never even made a pass at her.

Soon they were on the move again, this time to Pulau Bidong, a refugee camp where their ultimate destination would be determined.

Here My-Uyen, for the first time on her escape journey, felt the demons of imminent danger and strangulating fear recede toward the outer rim of awareness.

For here, to her great joy, she was reunited with her younger brother, Tom Cao, who had escaped Vietnam with his uncle two years earlier, but lacking the necessary papers, had not yet qualified for entry into the U.S.

My-Uyen spent twenty-five long days in this camp, keeping count by a ramen noodle for each day.

Still, the time passed more enjoyably now since she and her brother were at last together again.

There was much to talk about.

"I didn't expect to see you here," her brother told My-Uyen one day.

"Why not?"

"Because I tried to send warnings home that it wouldn't be safe."

"Of course it's dangerous, we all knew that."

"No, I don't mean just that. I told them not to send *you*."

"Because?"

"Because of what happens to young women. I've seen it. I've heard about it from many. I told them that you would be either raped or kidnapped, or both."

My-Uyen looked at her brother.

She understood.

Then she was silent.

When at last she spoke again, she said softly: "I knew about that, too. And I've been haunted by that fear all the way here. Somehow Dad and Mom must've felt that I would be safe. And somehow I must've trusted them, for otherwise I would not have come. Thanks, Brother, for caring."

Living conditions still left much to be desired.

My-Uyen, her brother, her uncle and his wife, and another woman had to share a living space barely large enough for six sleeping bags. They were rationed one bucket of water per person per day for cooking and bathing. Cooking was done on a primitive, rickety woodstove for which they had to gather the wood; and it had to be done by Muslim rules: no pork products, and no cooking past 7:00 p.m. Noodles were provided, and occasionally a small piece of chicken so tough that My-Uyen actually cracked her teeth on it. Sometimes they would venture out in a small group in the pitch dark with an oil lamp to try to catch fish and crab with a rudimentary net they had made from articles of clothing that had been donated. When they were successful, they feasted.

Finally the day came for their next move to another transitional camp, but this time much bigger and better.

The camp was in Sungai Besi, near Kuala Lumpur.

Here My-Uyen discovered what would mark her future life, though she did not yet know that.

She took under her wing two young boys of six and seven. One was light and the other dark. They became known simply as the white and the black boy.

My-Uyen asked her parents in a letter to contact the boys' parents; she included a picture of the boys. Her parents were able to impart the happy news to the boys' parents that they were alive and well with their daughter.

My-Uyen subsequently received a letter from the parents informing her that the boys' grandparents lived in Massachusetts, with a request to contact them regarding the boys' whereabouts.

This she did.

The grandparents were delighted to hear the good news and looking forward to welcoming the boys to their new home in the U.S.

A short time later, the boys were indeed on their way to their grandparents in Massachusetts.

It gave My-Uyen a high sense of fulfillment – helping others find the way, even as she was in the process of doing that for herself.

~~~

After two months at Kuala Lumpur, the time finally came for My-Uyen, her brother, and others to be sent on to the refugee camp in the Philippines, near Bataan. There they would be processed for resettlement in America, the land of freedom, a six-month process.

When they arrived at their new but temporary "home," they felt as if they had already taken the first step inside the Promised Land.

Living accommodations were still tight, but they had the entire outdoors to walk around in to regain a sense of individual freedom.

Food was better and more plentiful (though My-Uyen will always remember how hard the beans were), and sometimes people would share the food they bought at the market with money received from U.S. relatives.

Also, there was so much more to do here. There were activities and entertainment to keep them from getting bored, opportunities to join a religious group of their choice for social interaction (My-Uyen joined a young Buddhist group), and of course work, for each person was expected to put in a number of community hours each day.

Life quickly fell into a routine. Everyone had to take English language classes. My-Uyen's teacher was a tall young man from Massachusetts, so tall to the much shorter Vietnamese students, that they gave him the nickname "giraffe." But the students liked him, especially because he treated them to chocolate after the break.

English translators were badly needed, so many students were checked for possible qualification.

My-Uyen did not want that job, for she had heard that it was grueling work with long hours.

When it became her turn to be checked for possible
~~~

qualification, she was determined to play dumb.

She sat down across from the English teacher, trying to concentrate on not betraying her knowledge of English that she had accumulated during the last four to five years of private tutoring in Vietnam.

"Hello, what's your name?"

A slight shake of the head.

"How old are you?"

That's easy. Give him a blank look.

"How long have you been here?"

Okay, concentrate. He's tricky. Just stare back.

"Do you like it here?"

Watch it, you were almost going to nod yes. Don't shake it either. Just frown. Good. "Do you understand English?"

"Me no English."

Oops! Now you did it, you blew it!

My-Uyen claps her hand over her mouth, but the unguarded words are out. There's nothing to do now but to laugh about it, and they do.

She leaves with the words, "You've got yourself a job," ringing in her ears.

It turned out that My-Uyen enjoyed the work as translator for the English class. She was needed especially when the teacher tried to teach students about American culture and history, which tended to be beyond the linguistic competency level of most students. As she exercised the English skills she had, her own facility with the language also began to improve.

There was another Papa here, but this one was a good Papa. He, too, had escaped Vietnam, having been employed by the Americans during the war. He had even come to the U.S. in 1969 to get trained for his work with the American military.

But he would reveal nothing about his personal life, likely fearful that the communists would find a way to take revenge on the family and relatives left in Vietnam.

He took her and her brother under his wing and showed them much kindness.

Since the refugees earned no money, they were completely dependent on what people would give them. Papa gave My-Uyen money for stamps every week so she could mail letters to her parents. Papa also warned them which parts of the camp to avoid because of drug activity.

He was a devout Roman Catholic, and his Christian caretaking left a deep impression on My-Uyen. Later she would think of him as an angel sent from heaven.

~~~

My-Uyen and her brother had been in the Philippines for nearly seven months now.

They knew they would soon get word that their time had come for departure.

One day My-Uyen received a letter from her parents with the address of a former classmate who now lived in Texas. She wrote that friend. The friend wrote back and included a twenty-dollar bill with the letter, intended as a little travel money for the trip to the U.S.

Two weeks later brother and sister were on their way.

They were headed for Grand Rapids, Michigan, a place they had been told would be very cold. They did not know exactly what that meant, for they had never been very cold.

In fact, they did not really know anything about the future waiting for them, a future that had only been a remote promise and a kind of impossible dream for so long.

Part of them felt an ecstatic state of disbelief that it was really going to happen; part of them felt a rising wave of anxiety about an unknown future.

But they had each other, and the comfort of knowing that their parents' hopes and love would follow them all the way.

When the plane finally touched down at the Grand
~~~

Rapids airport, the two travel-weary refugees saw a snow-covered world for the first time in their lives.

It was March 31, 1987, and in West Michigan still very far from springtime.

They couldn't help but shiver when the first blast of winter air hit them as they disembarked through the passenger boarding bridge.

But they soon forgot about winter when they were warmly welcomed by people from Trinity, the church that would be their official sponsor.

One was a young man with a very hairy face that made My-Uyen wonder momentarily whether she was meeting a member of the Ape Family she had learned about as our human ancestors.

And when she saw people pick up her luggage and started carrying it away, she chased after them and fought to regain her suitcase, thinking that surely these people must be thieves.

Strange faces, a strange culture, a strange language they were still learning – it was all too overwhelming, but she was learning, safely so, and that would make all the difference to the two young people who had braved many dangers and even death since their escape from Vietnam.

Still, when they at last were ready to leave for the parking lot, the bitterly cold wind hit in full force, slicing into their tropical climate pores like the cold steel of a scimitar. My-Uyen once again thought she would be facing death.

The irony struck her as ludicrous, but she was sure that here, in the Promised Land, the cold that was freezing her inside and out would surely kill her.

But it was warm when she was ushered inside her new home in a suburb of Grand Rapids.

Here she was welcomed with open arms into a new family, with a new "Dad" and "Mom" and siblings.

They eagerly showed her around her new "home," including her own bedroom.

This would be her new life.

That night, exhausted, My-Uyen fell into a long and dreamless sleep.

When at last she woke at midmorning the next day, her new siblings enticed her to come out and build a snowman with them.

It was her first act of bonding with her new family and with her snow-covered new country.

To her surprise and relief, she discovered that, again, she would not die.

She felt the fear that had tightened her chest again and again for too long begin to deflate.

~~~

My-Uyen's parents had wanted greater educational opportunities for their bright young daughter.

They had risked her safety, even her life, for that dream.

And now that dream was becoming a reality.

My-Uyen graduated from Calvin Christian High School in Grandville, went on to Grand Rapids Community College, then transferred to Dordt College, a Christian College in Northwest Iowa, and eventually went on to earn her MSW degree from Grand Valley State University near Grand Rapids.

Her parents had hoped with all their heart that their daughter would find a good home to look after her, a good school to educate her, and then a good position to provide her with a good living.

She did.

But what they had not anticipated was that their daughter would also find and embrace the Christian faith in her new home and school and church.

Before she graduated from high school, My-Uyen gave her life to Christ, was baptized, made public profession of her faith in the sponsoring church, and vowed from henceforth to live her life in loving service to the God who saved her and to
~~~

others in need of help as she once was.

She is keeping that vow. My-Uyen occupies a spacious, attractive office as a Refugee Services Supervisor for Bethany Christian Service in Grand Rapids, Michigan. She offers counseling and support to refugees who struggle to find their way in a strange country and culture in which they often feel alienated.

It is her calling, a calling she felt moving within her already when she reached out to others who needed her on the "big fish" and in the refugee camp.

And she has not forgotten the land and the people she left behind.

Many a summer, in her vacation time, My-Uyen, with her husband and two children, flies back to Vietnam.

One summer her American family went with them.

Among them they took 1,000 pounds of luggage loaded with supplies.

They visited the homeless in their shelters, the hungry, the indigent and elderly, the mentally ill, the orphans.

They brought gifts of clothing, basic supplies, food, and the love of God into the lives of people who suffer from loneliness, emptiness, and hopelessness.

My-Uyen and her own family continue to go on this mission of mercy, ministering to "the least of these" in the name of the Lord who saved her for such service.

No, My-Uyen has not forgotten her people in the country of her birth.

Neither has she forgotten the treacherous journey that brought her to America.

Often she speaks to church groups about that time in 1986 when she left everything behind in the hope of reaching the dreams for a better life.

She tells them, too, how she expected more than once never to see her family again.

She talks passionately and poignantly about those harrowing experiences.

But every time she comes to the part in her flight from Vietnam where she missed her step, she chokes up.

The mystery of that strong hand which lifted her to safety is still a mystery.

But to My-Uyen, that mystery now strikes her more as a miracle, as the saving Hand of God Himself literally snatching her from the jaws of death.

And the thought of Almighty God, whom she has come to love, stooping down to catch her because He loved her even then, is enough to dissolve her in tears of humble gratitude.

Gratitude for her new life in the new country.

But much more than that, gratitude for her new life in Christ, of which she never tires to testify.

The Author of Miracles

Once more, Dan walked around his airplane, which he had parked on a small grass landing strip in Long Beach, Washington. It was a thirty-year-old Cessna model 175, which the company no longer manufactured. National accident statistics indicated that during its thirty years, the Cessna 175 had not accumulated a stellar safety record. Cessna had eventually replaced it with the Skylane 182.

Dan never failed to read aviation accident reports. He knew that above-average incidents of engine failures were well-known. He also knew that many of those failures were due to improper maintenance and even improper pilot technique in managing engine power settings. For today's flight, Dan had already checked the oil, the tires, and the free movement of ailerons, flaps, rudder, and elevator. He was a professional commercial pilot and maintained his airplane without ever "cutting corners." He had never experienced any problems of any kind with his airplane. That was important, because his clientele often included government officials and CEOs of large companies.

He looked at his watch. His client should be arriving shortly.

~~~

It had been a long day for Bob Williams. After serving
~~~

as a legislator in Washington State for ten years, he was now in the midst of a hotly contested, adrenaline-pumping campaign for governor. He made one speech after another, day after day, often into the late evening hours. His throngs of loyal supporters attended his appearances in various parts of the state. At the conclusion of his campaign speeches, many members of the audience rushed forward to shake the candidate's hand and express their well wishes. Fortunately, candidate Williams was blessed with boundless energy.

Today, however, as he rode in the backseat of the car driven by a campaign aide, he felt drained. He tried to relax during the ride to the small private airstrip where a four-seat Cessna was waiting to return him to Olympia, the state capital. He hoped to arrive while it was still daylight so he would have time to go over the speeches he'd be making the next day to the Republican conventions in King and Snohomish Counties.

As the car pulled up beside the waiting airplane, the pilot, Dan, exited and walked around the front of the plane to open Bob's car door. Moving to the Cessna 175, Bob settled into the co-pilot seat. By the time Dan had finished his walk-around inspection, Bob had put his briefcase in the backseat and, as usual, donned the co-pilot headphones that enabled him to converse with the pilot. He felt an uncharacteristic weariness and would have preferred to just sit back quietly and not wear the headphones. But that would send a message to his friend Dan that he wasn't in the mood to talk. Being "unfriendly" was not an ingredient of Bob's personality.

The engine started, and Dan began his pre-flight routine. He placed both feet firmly on the brakes before revving up the engine to maximum rpm. Then he carefully observed any significant drop in rpm as he switched from left to right magneto. After reducing the engine power to idle, he checked for proper movement of control surfaces, made sure Bob's seatbelt was securely fastened, and turned the airplane in a full 360-degree circle while scanning the sky for possible conflicting traffic.

"Okay, Mr. Williams, let's head for Olympia," Dan said.

Bob gave him the thumbs-up signal as engine power was increased to maximum, and within twenty seconds they were airborne. Within a few minutes, the airplane had climbed to 3,000 feet and was cruising in a northerly direction at about 130 miles per hour.

Bob adjusted his microphone close to his lips. "Dan," he said, "we've covered the three hundred or so miles from the north of the state to the south a few times already, with numerous stops in between. This seems to be a reliable airplane, and you're a good pilot."

"Well, thank you, Mr. Williams. It's always a pleasure getting you from one appearance to another. I've got a few thousand flying hours in my logbook, and yes, this old Cessna has been a pretty reliable workhorse."

"How old is it?" Bob asked.

"Thirty years. Cessna quit manufacturing this model in the early sixties."

"How about the twin-engine we use when you fly me across the Cascades to eastern Washington?"

"Good question," said Dan. "We won't fly customers across the mountain range in a single-engine airplane. We use a Piper Apache. It's not a new airplane either, but it is equipped with two 180-horsepower Lycoming engines. It originally came out with two 150-horsepower engines, and it was often called a '3,500-pound toad.'"

Bob laughed and repeated the word "toad."

"Well," said Dan, "actually it's not a glamorous-looking airplane, but with the two 180-horsepower engines, it's a great performer. It has de-icing wing boots, and we can heat the prop in case we encounter icing conditions over the mountains."

"Is that fairly common?"

"During fall, winter, and early spring, it's not a rare

occasion. We take icing conditions very seriously, and we've never been caught by surprise."

"Hey, look," said Bob, pointing straight ahead. "Is that the Olympia airport?"

"Yes it is, Mr. Williams. I'd better begin losing some altitude."

He retarded the throttle just a little. Promptly the engine coughed, and the cockpit became very quiet.

While the propeller was still windmilling, Dan did his best to restart the engine. He pumped the throttle, adjusted the mixture control to full "rich," and as quickly as the engine had fallen silent, it now roared back to life. Bob relaxed as he watched Dan adjust the flaps for final approach.

Again the engine coughed, sputtered, and quit. This time it refused to start despite Dan's best efforts. Bob stared out through the windshield at the airport runway lights, an impossible distance away. Then the Cessna lurched as one of its wings brushed the upper limbs of a tree.

"We're going down!" Dan yelled. "Brace yourself –"

~~~

Everything is "normal" during the first few years of a child's life. Bob Williams was unaware that he was born in one of the most impoverished areas in Pennsylvania and perhaps in the country. He was unaware of the reality that it was difficult for his mother to feed four children. He was unaware of the absence of a father. For an infant, things are "normal" just as they are. A young child has no basis for comparisons.

That begins to change after only a few short years. Bob was about five years old when he said to his mom, "Where is Dad, Mommy?"

She gazed at him silently. He noticed tears pooling in her eyes. She looked so sad, and he was sorry he had asked a question that was clearly very painful for her to answer.

She sat in a chair next to her son and took his hand. Tears now trickled down her cheeks. "Bobby, I'm so sorry. Your daddy died in a tragic accident when you were only nine
~~~

months old. He was a good man and a wonderful dad and a good husband. He was a good provider. We always had enough to eat." She looked out the kitchen window. "You'll never know him. I was only twenty-five years old with four children and no means of support. We can barely get enough food on the help we get from welfare. There's never any money for clothes for you kids."

At the age of five, Bob couldn't understand the plight of a near-destitute mother as he watched her bury her face in her arms resting on the table.

"Bobby, I don't know what to do," she sobbed. "I pray every day, but I feel helpless and hopeless."

Bob started crying, too. He had just received a glimpse of abject poverty.

When he started school, he began to understand that his family must be very poor. Kids at school teased him about wearing ill-fitting, hand-me-down clothes.

Mom had told his brother that she would have to send him and Bob to a Christian boarding school for fatherless boys – an orphanage. Bob was eight years old when his mom dropped him off at the school. She looked sad but didn't say anything. He didn't remember her giving him a hug or a kiss. He only remembered that he was devastated.

An eight-year-old was too young to understand the plight of a single, widowed mother who tried to supplement her small welfare check by working for ten dollars a week. Her four children were growing up, and she must have known that she would be unable to provide for their needs. She may have sent her two boys to a good Christian facility because she felt insecure about raising two sons without the presence of a father.

At that time, none of those thoughts occurred to Bob. He knew only that he was at a boarding school for fatherless boys.

Maybe Mother knew what was best for her sons. At the school, he learned about Jesus and His love and became very close to his Savior. The boys were also taught the value of money and work. In order to raise spending money, Bob chose to go door-to-door selling magazine subscriptions. He was quite successful and learned something about persuasion.

One day he knocked on the door of one especially beautiful home. An equally beautiful car was parked in the driveway. He had butterflies in his stomach, like he did every time he knocked on a door. Soon the door opened, and he found himself looking up at a large, well-dressed man.

"Sir," Bob began, "I live at Girard College, a boarding school for fatherless boys. To earn spending money, I sell magazine subscriptions."

Instead of closing the door in his face, the man asked, "What kind of magazines do you sell, young man?"

Bob pulled a magazine out of his small leather folder and handed it to the man. "Sir, I have a great special on a three-year subscription to the Saturday Evening Post," he said enthusiastically. "Not only will you get dozens of great stories, but every issue also has a beautiful painting by Norman Rockwell on the glossy front cover."

The man invited Bob into his house while he wrote a check made out to the Saturday Evening Post for a three-year subscription. Shaking his outstretched hand, Bob thanked him profusely.

When Bob was fourteen years old, something very unusual happened. He didn't know if any of his teachers had recommended him because he was a serious, hard-working student, or if it was providential. His life would change forever.

Bob was sitting on a bench admiring the manicured grounds of the Girard school, enjoying the peaceful summer Sunday afternoon. Other than food preparation activities, Sunday was a day of rest. Silhouetted against the blue sky, a flock of birds was flying south, probably on their early migration route. He was in a contemplative mood, and his thoughts went to the worship service he'd attended in the morning. The visiting pastor had known that his audience wasn't an average congregation. He'd known he was speaking exclusively to fatherless children.

Bob thought about the little his mother had told him about his father. Yes, she had told him that his father had really loved him, and that he'd often held and kissed him when he was just a tiny baby. Now, as he was getting older, he often longed to know his father. But he knew it would never happen during his lifetime. Again he looked up to the pale blue skies. All he knew from the pastor's message this morning was that his heavenly father was there, and that He would never leave him or forsake him.

Bob's reveries were interrupted when a big, gleaming car drove up the short driveway and stopped at the front door of the school. He thought he recognized the well-dressed gentleman who exited the car. Maybe he was a friend or relative of the school's headmaster. Then it dawned on him. Yes, he had seen this man before. That was the same beautiful car. Yes, he was the man who had bought a three-year magazine subscription from Bob.

The man noticed him sitting on the bench and waved as he recognized him. Impressed, Bob waved back. Minutes later, the man walked toward him with the schoolmaster. Nervously, Bob wondered what they might want.

The headmaster said, "Bob, this is Mr. Klomar, and he has a question."

Bob jumped up and extended his right hand. "I'm glad to meet you again, Mr. Klomar."

The man smiled and gave Bob a firm handshake. "Hi, Bob, I'm glad to meet you again, too. I just asked your headmaster for permission to invite you to our house this evening for dinner, and he approved. Would you like to do that?"

The unexpected invitation didn't require a second thought. Bob nodded his head vigorously. "Yes, sir!"

A short time later, he was sitting at a very long dinner

table with Mr. and Mrs. Klomar and their thirteen children. It was the first time in his life that he had sat around a dinner table with a complete family. Not only was the dinner delicious, the whole experience was impressive. The Klomar family would have an enormous impact on Bob's life.

Mr. Klomar took him under his wing and unofficially adopted him as his fourteenth child. He found jobs for Bob to do during his Christmas and summer breaks and encouraged him to go to college. As far as Bob knew, no one in the entire Williams family had ever attended college. The Klomar family made it possible for Bob to attend college and even paid some of the costs. He soon received a four-year scholarship covering his tuition at the prestigious State University of Pennsylvania. While at the university, Bob joined the Reserve Officers Training Corps (ROTC). In order to pay for his meals, he worked in the dining room.

As a youngster at Girard College, Bob had learned all the regular school subjects. But he'd also learned about subjects he had never given much thought to before. He learned about the founding principles of America, the Declaration of Independence, the Constitution, and the Bill of Rights. Most importantly, he had learned about Jesus and His love, and he became very close to his Savior. Bob could not have known then that these two subjects would profoundly influence his life. He could not have known how passionate he would become about honesty and righteousness in government, personal responsibility, and serving God each and every day of his journey through life.

~~~

Lieutenant Bob Williams was on guard duty one bitterly cold October night at the Army base in Nuremberg, Germany, when, a little after ten o'clock, a young woman dressed as a hippie approached him holding a steaming cup of coffee.

She handed him the cup. "Hello, Lieutenant," she said. "The club just closed. This is from Sergeant Wolfe. He thought you might need it."
~~~

Bob was a bit bewildered as he accepted the coffee. Then he remembered that the enlisted soldiers' service club was holding a Halloween party that night. That explained the costume.

The young woman's name was Jane. She intrigued Bob, and over the next few weeks he found himself frequently visiting the officers' club where she worked. She remembered him, and they often engaged in small talk over a cup of coffee.

"Lieutenant Williams . . . "

Bob interrupted her. "Jane, why don't you just call me Bob?"

She studied him seriously for a few seconds before smiling. "Okay, Bob."
Sitting across the table from him, she began telling him that she would be going on a tour to Israel in March.

Bob interrupted. "You're going on one of the Holy Land tours?"

She nodded with enthusiasm. "I'm sure I'll get to see the places and maybe even walk where Jesus walked two thousand years ago."

Now it was Bob's turn to study Jane more intently. "Jane, are you a Christian?" He didn't really have to ask. Her excitement about getting to "walk where Jesus walked" had already confirmed that she was a believer.

However, Jane needed no prompting to answer his question. "Yes, Lieutenant– oops, Bob. I'm a Christian." After a brief moment of hesitation, she asked, "Are you?"

"Yes, I really am," he replied. "I love my Savior, and I'm scheduled on the February tour to Israel."

Jane was awe-struck. They continued their relaxed conversation until he looked at his watch and realized that it was past time for him to return to his military officer duties.

~~~

For much of that night, sleep eluded him. He couldn't get Jane out of his mind. Yes, he knew that women were up-
~~~

permost in the minds of most soldiers. His mental activity didn't revolve around women, however. He had never seriously dated any girl, and based on what he heard from soldiers about their "conquests," he didn't hold those standards of morality in high regard. Jane was different. She was a Christian. While her faith was still in its infancy, she was honest and believed that her devotion to God should be reflected in every aspect of her life. Yes, she was a very attractive young lady. It was her faith and the strength of her character that he admired, and they became good friends.

Jane didn't want their relationship to blossom into anything beyond friendship. She was engaged to a tall, handsome soldier. She had been attracted to the man because of his looks and his sophisticated, worldly ways. Bob had no intention of allowing his relationship with Jane to grow beyond just being good friends. But he knew Jane was a good Christian lady, and based on what she had told him about the man she was engaged to, he didn't think this man was one she should regard as a compatible, God-fearing life partner. As he lay there awake, he prayed that God would make Jane see that.

Now his restless dreams took him back to his college days when he had been in the ROTC in the regular Army. Though he had no intention of making the military his lifetime career, he'd enjoyed taking advantage of every opportunity available for advancement. He was curious, energetic, aggressive, and adventuresome. When he'd learned that it was possible to earn his Army Airborne Wings, he had immediately volunteered. It required several hours of classroom instruction during the first week. Successfully completing the test qualified students to advance to the second week. During the second week, they had to practice jumps from a 34-foot tower without a parachute. It simulated the very solid contact with the ground they would experience when landing with a parachute, without breaking bones. Then came "Jump Week." He had learned the importance of packing his parachute. He knew that a mistake would likely cost him his life.

Suddenly, Bob was wide-awake in his bunk in Nuremberg, drenched with perspiration. Another dream about that first jump had renewed in him an intense fear.

Daylight filtered through the drapes. It was time to get up. He found himself chuckling. *Strange how dreams can be so real*, he thought. In retrospect, it was funny. He'd have to tell Jane the story of his first jump the next time he saw her at the club.

~~~

The next morning, Bob sat at his desk preparing to check his list of activities and responsibilities for the day. Reliving his dream of last night, he had difficulty concentrating. Deep in thought, he looked out the window. Large, fluffy snowflakes were descending, all landing softly on the ground, which would soon be covered with a pure white blanket that would transform the scenery into a winter wonderland.

Returning his attention to the papers on his desk, Bob sighed. Just as he was beginning to concentrate on his task, the telephone rang.

"Hello, is this Lieutenant Williams?" It was a voice he didn't recognize.

"Yes, sir, Lieutenant Williams here."

"My name is Wilhelm, and I'm with Hill Holy Land Tours. Our records show that you are scheduled on our February tour. Is that correct, sir?"

Enthusiastically Bob responded, "Yes, sir, and I'm really looking forward to it."

"I'm sorry, sir, but I'm afraid our February tour has been cancelled due to insufficient participation."

Shocked and disappointed, Bob fell silent.

Wilhelm didn't let the silence linger. "But I have good news, too," he said.

"What's the good news?"

"We have a few seats available on our March tour. But of course I don't know if that will work for you."
~~~

"Okay, Wilhelm, give me a minute. Let me check."

Right away, Bob knew he'd be able to adjust his schedule. In the next instant, he remembered that March was the month Jane was scheduled on the tour. He felt a strange sense of excitement as he picked up the phone again. "Okay, Wilhelm, I can make that work," he said, while doing his level best to prevent the excitement from being reflected in his voice.

While performing his required activities of the day, Bob tried to concentrate on his tasks. His mind wandered frequently. He couldn't shed that feeling of excitement. Deep inside, he knew that he didn't really want to, either. He longed for evening to come. Visiting with Jane at the officers' club was something he looked forward to, especially now that he knew he'd be on the same Holy Land tour she was booked on. He also wanted to tell Jane about his first jump out of an airplane. He put on his dress uniform. It even displayed the impressive Airborne Wing, identifying him has a member of the elite Paratroop division.

~~~

Bob arrived at the service club early. He was glad when he noticed that it wasn't busy. It meant that Jane would have free time to chat. He looked around and noticed she was serving some officers in the far corner of the club with her back toward Bob. He seated himself at a table some distance from where Jane was serving.

He had never thought of himself as being even remotely in love with Jane. He'd never been in love with a girlfriend or even considered it. As he was watching her, he couldn't help thinking how pretty she was, moving so smoothly and gracefully from one table to another, always wearing that beautiful, friendly smile.

It wasn't long before Jane noticed that she had another customer to serve. Being in his dress uniform some distance from where she was working, Bob could tell that she didn't recognize him. He quickly removed his formal officer's cap
~~~

with the shiny visor and waved. Now Jane recognized him immediately and, wearing that broad smile, quickly approached his table. With a surprised look on her face, she said, "Wow, Lieutenant Williams are you ever looking sharp!"

Bob stood up and extended his hand for a handshake. "Jane, I'm still Bob to you."

Jane looked at him up and down, and her eyes settled on his silver wing insignia. "You look fantastic. Are you a pilot?"

He smiled. "No. That decoration identifies me as having passed my schooling and tests as a paratrooper. In fact, I wanted to tell you about my first jump out of an airplane."

Jane sat down in the chair opposite him. "I'd love to hear that."

Bob settled back in his chair, cleared his throat, and said, "Okay, Jane. I'll start with the end."

"Why start with the end?"

"Because then you'll know that I was more scared then I'd ever been in my life." Now he had Jane's full attention. "The jumpmaster observed us packing our parachutes. In ground school, we were impressed with the fact that one small error in packing our chutes could be fatal.

"I'm sure we were at least a mile high into the air when we lined up by the exit door. A few fellow cadets were ahead of me, but we followed each other in rapid succession, jumping into the void. I jumped, and as I counted to three before pulling the ripcord, I saw several parachutes already blossoming below on their way to terra firma. I was ready for that enormous jolt we had been prepared for when our chutes deployed. I felt the jolt, but it wasn't as bad as I expected. At least I knew that my equipment had been properly packed. It was what happened next that was completely beyond my understanding, and totally inconsistent with everything I'd been taught.

"Instead of floating downward, I was going *up*! Soon I

saw the plane, which I had just exited, below me instead of above me. My heart was pounding in my chest. Yes, I fully expected to go to heaven after my earthly work was done and life was over, but I wasn't ready to go there just yet."

Jane exploded in spontaneous laughter at Bob's suggestion that he'd thought he was ascending into heaven. Then she stopped abruptly. Bob had said that he'd experienced the scariest moments of his life. She seemed to realize it was altogether inappropriate for her to laugh. Quickly she wiped the smile from her face and replaced it with an expression of concern.

"That must have been real scary," she said. "But I'm looking at you, so I know you made it down safely. Tell me what happened. How did you make it down?"

Bob was still studying Jane. *She's beautiful*, he thought. Then he quickly banished those thoughts from his mind and responded to her question. "I was still gaining altitude when I heard a powerful voice from the next airplane below, yelling my name. I wanted to think it was the voice of God, but it didn't come from on high. The voice, amplified by a powerful megaphone, yelled, 'Hey, Williams, don't worry. You *will* come down. You got caught in an updraft. Don't worry, you'll be fine!'

"Well, I did come down, a little quickly at first as the updraft changed into a downdraft. As I saw earth approaching fast, I bent my knees, pulled the flare cords with all my strength, and made a perfect touchdown."

They both laughed as he finished the story.

"I have more to share with you," he said. He now had a serious expression on his face, and Jane listened intently. "The German tour agency cancelled the Israel tour I was booked on in February."

Jane's hands flew to her cheeks as she exclaimed, "Oh no! You were really looking forward to that tour as a spiritual journey. I'm so sorry to hear that."

As he listened to Jane and saw the sincerity in her face,

he couldn't escape thinking again how pretty she was. A nearly imperceptible, mischievous smile curled his lips slightly. Then his expression turned serious again. "You're right. It would be an important spiritual journey for me, but it's also very important to you, isn't it?'

"Oh, definitely. I feel kind of bad, because a spiritual journey isn't at all important to my fiancé. Of course, he's not going, either."

Bob remained silent for what seemed like minutes. When he spoke, he placed his elbows on the table and looked Jane squarely in the eye.

"Jane, your handsome fiancé is not on the same spiritual wavelength you are on. It worries me. You're my friend, and if I can help it, I want the best for all my friends. Of course, that's not in my hands. But I really would want you to be able to live a long, joyful life in the Lord."

Now it was Jane's turn to stare at Bob silently, trying to read his expression. "I appreciate your concern, Bob, but it'll be just fine."

Bob got the message. It was time to change the subject. He smiled at Jane and said, "I still have more news."

That triggered her curiosity. "I hope it's good," she said, looking at him expectantly.

"It's good. I was excited. The fellow from the tour company, Wilhelm, said they had a vacancy on the March tour and asked if that would work for me. I checked my schedule, made a couple of phone calls, and presto, I'll be on the same tour you're scheduled on. Isn't that amazing?'

Jane waited a moment before responding. When she finally spoke, her voice carried a tone of caution. "Yes, that is amazing. I'm happy for you. But remember, I'm engaged."

"Okay, Jane, I hear you. Let me put your mind at ease. You're afraid that I might have romantic designs on you. Maybe you'll find this hard to believe, but it's the truth. I've never thought of you as my girlfriend, just a good friend. In fact, I've never actually *had* a girlfriend. I've never kissed a woman romantically. I know most guys my age are obsessed with girlfriends. Yes, I hope to have a wife and family someday, but my primary focus right now is how I can be an effective ambassador for my Savior and how I can best serve the country I love."

Jane smiled at Bob, then reached across the table, and placed her hand on top of his hand. Their eyes met as she said, "You're a good man, Lieutenant Williams." It was as if an electric current coursed through his body as her hand rested on his.

Before Bob could respond, she'd left to return to her duties.

~~~

All sixty-four pilgrims on tour in Israel were silent. They were attending an open-air Good Friday service in Jerusalem. The sky was gray. Rain threatened.

When the pastor got to the part when Jesus came forth from his tomb, the clouds dissipated, and this impressive service and all those attending were bathed in brilliant sunlight.

For Bob, another unforgettable experience came when they walked along the route Jesus had taken on His way to the cross. Bob and the others walked along the Via Dolorosa, stopping at the Lithostrotos pavement where Pilate had sentenced Jesus to death. They walked the areas where the cross had stood until they arrived at the Church of the Holy Sepulcher, the likely site of the crucifixion near the tomb of Christ.

For both Bob and Jane, the experiences of the Holy Land tour strengthened their faith and would enrich their spiritual journey for the rest of their lives.

Even though Jane was on the same tour, Bob had little interaction with her. The tour was not conducive to romance. The men slept in a different hotel from the women. It was still a time of segregation. Whenever Jane felt that Bob was getting a little "chummy," she would quickly remind him that she was engaged.
~~~

A strong camaraderie had developed among the sixty-four members of the tour. They began to know each other well, as they spent every day of the tour together and experienced the awesome sights of this land so incredibly rich with ancient history. It was no surprise that everyone knew Jane would be celebrating her twenty-fifth birthday in Israel.

The details of the planned celebration were not disclosed to Jane. She had no idea that they were preparing sixty-four small cakes, all artistically decorated with her name in letters made of frosting. She was surprised when she was asked to mount a camel, not realizing that it would be led to the site of her birthday party.

For some reason, Bob was selected to present the first small cake to Jane. What happened next was not something he had planned. As he offered the cake to her, the words just seemed to bubble up from somewhere deep inside him.

"Jane," he said, keeping his eyes fixed on hers, "let's make this your birthday party . . . and our engagement party."

To his everlasting surprise, she smiled and said, "Okay, Bob, it's my birthday and our engagement party."

For the rest of their lives, they would always remember that evening as a miracle from God.

~~~

After a whirlwind three-and-a-half month romance, Bob and Jane were married in the city where Jane had been born and raised: Tacoma, Washington. Once Bob had finished his military service as a captain in Fort Lee, Virginia, they moved on to Washington, D.C., for Bob's new civilian position at the U.S. Government Accountability Office.

While Bob and Jane were happily married, it became increasingly apparent that Jane was lonely. She had been born in the beautiful state of Washington, near the shores of the Pacific Ocean, where her parents and family lived. That was where all her childhood memories had originated, where friendships had been forged and experiences shared. Even though Bob's childhood had been vastly different from
~~~

Jane's, he understood that the area of her birth beckoned with increasing intensity. Bob loved his wife and wanted her to be happy.

After a few short years in Washington, D.C., Bob and Jane moved to the southwestern area of Washington State. He had secured a position with Weyerhaeuser as a log accountability officer. His duties, which involved keeping track of the number of logs cut and when and where the logs were shipped, required working in a small office in the forest. During breaks, he would stand in the woods listening to the birds sing and watching the leaves flutter in the breeze. Enjoying this beautiful symphony of nature, he could meditate and observe the majesty of God's creation while dreaming about the future. He prayed that his passion for politics would someday become a reality.

His prayers were answered when he was asked to work as the campaign manager for an incumbent state legislator. He managed a successful campaign, and his friend was reelected. When the legislator decided not to run again, Bob had the opportunity to run for the position. He campaigned tirelessly. Against enormous odds, with his beloved Jane as his biggest cheerleader, he won and served in the state government for the next ten years.

~~~

Lee Hensley looked at his watch. It was nearly 10:00 p.m. He'd been driving the eighteen-wheeler Peterbilt tractor-trailer all day. He was tired, and he knew that he should have stopped at the previous rest area, parked his truck, and crawled into the cab's comfortable sleeping quarters. He would have, except the big engine needed service, and it was only a few more miles north on I-5 where he would exit the freeway and park his truck at the factory-authorized Western Peterbilt company in Fife, Washington. He could then walk less then two blocks and afford himself the luxury of sleeping in a nice motel room. All the arrangements were already made. His full load would be delivered to a Vancouver, B.C.,
~~~

warehouse the following day.

Driving along I-5 through the Tacoma area, he started paying attention to the exits. He would have to leave the interstate freeway at Exit 137. He was still speeding along the left lane when he noticed the sign informing him that the next exit would be #137, with an arrow pointing to the right. It was less than a mile.

Immediately, he flipped his right directional signal on and took his foot off the accelerator while quickly checking his rearview mirror. Traffic was still heavy, and he became concerned when he realized that he would have to navigate across three lanes of traffic in a short distance. Missing the proper exit was a possibility he didn't even want to think about. He'd just have to be carefully aggressive, he told himself as he eased the big rig into the adjoining lane.

With his right turn signal blinking, he kept checking his rearview mirror. Yes, traffic was just short of bumper-to-bumper, but he knew that all the vehicles visible in his large mirror could see his flashing turn signal. As he squeezed into the next lane, he was quite sure that no other driver would be eager to tangle with a big eighteen-wheeler. *Only one more lane to go.*

Though he couldn't know it at the time, from now on he would never again forget that whenever he looked in the rearview mirror, there was a small blind spot. Nor would he ever forget the hair-raising events of the next few moments and the terrifying sound of metal scraping on metal.

~~~

Bob rarely went to important functions without Jane. He valued her feedback and critique. Bob had an important political speech he was scheduled to deliver before a large audience in Seattle. They left their home in Olympia a little early for several reasons, among which was the normally heavy freeway traffic. It also allowed them to drive in the slow lane, giving Bob the opportunity to discuss the main points of his speech with Jane. It almost always resulted in
~~~

Bob making some refinements to his speech.

Never switching lanes and cruising along at a leisurely 55 miles per hour, they also had ample time to talk about their three sons. Two had already reached adulthood, and their youngest was not far behind. Bob and Jane often talked about their family and the blessings and challenges of parenthood.

Bob had an exciting career in politics, with never a dull moment during the ten years he'd served in the state legislature. He was recognized nationwide for his fierce sense of integrity, individual responsibility, and no-waste fiscal conservatism. Now he was campaigning for the position of governor of the state. This was much different from seeking a position as a legislator, which required covering only one relatively small district. Jane remembered Bob wearing out several pairs of shoes covering the towns in his district door-to-door on foot. This, on the other hand, was the entire state of Washington and just the start of a long campaign – a daunting task for anyone except Bob. He was enthusiastic and energetic.

Jane was looking at the heavy traffic when she said, "Bob, don't you often wonder where everyone is going?"

Bob looked to his left, where vehicles in the faster lanes were constantly passing. "Wherever it is, they always seem to be in a hurry to get there." Grinning, he glanced at Jane. "Let's assume they're all heading for the grand ballroom of the Luxor Hotel to hear my speech, and they want to make sure there'll be a seat when they arrive."

They were both laughing now, when out of his peripheral vision Bob became aware of a large truck crowding them. He didn't have time to look, but it seemed closer than it should be. Even though it was in the faster lane, it was slowing, and Bob pressed on the accelerator to get ahead of this big rig as quickly as possible. He was almost ahead of it when their world turned upside down.

They heard the sickening crunch of metal-on-metal and felt an enormous bump that spun them around. An instant later, Bob and Jane were staring straight through the windshield at the cab of the big truck. Had this occurred in slow motion, they would have seen the bewildered driver sitting behind the wheel.

A second collision was unavoidable, and they were tossed into the adjoining lane. Turning 360 degrees, they came to a stop facing oncoming traffic. Brakes and tires screamed as vehicles skidded, coming to a screeching halt at crazy angles. For a brief moment, it was very quiet. Bob and Jane unlatched their seatbelts and exited the bent, twisted wreck that had been their car.

Without a word, they walked to the berm alongside the freeway. It didn't require conversation for both of them to know that they had just been given another miracle from on high.

~~~

Bob sat behind his desk, staring out the window without noticing the beauty of the late summer day. Several months had passed since that frightening day on the freeway. His mind was preoccupied, which was understandable. Tonight he was to give the most important campaign speech of his career. He was running for governor against a popular incumbent. It was late in the campaign. He'd been working on his speech for days.

But that was not what occupied his mind as he stared vacantly through his office window. A plan had developed when he realized that he would have to pull his thoughts away from his reveries and concentrate on refining his speech.

He picked up the draft of his speech and began to review it.

> *We don't need tax reform; we need tax control. We don't need spending reform; we need spending control. We don't need budget reform; we need budget control. We don't need welfare reform; we need welfare con-*
~~~

> *trol. Accountability and responsibility are what every citizen of the state has a right to expect from its government and all the agencies that serve them.*

Bob pondered again. Both elbows rested on the desktop, his chin cradled in his hands.

He had served in the legislature for ten years. Most citizens with any interest in state politics knew what he stood for. They knew about his straightforward honesty. They knew he had always insisted on fiscal responsibility. They knew about the values and principles that guided him in his personal life as well as his work as a legislator.

But he was also certain that there were important aspects of his life they didn't know about. Tonight he would change that.

~~~

Bob squinted into the bright spotlights but couldn't really see much beyond the glare. The applause was deafening. All he knew was that he had a very large audience.

Then his eyes focused on Jane, a small woman in the front row. On an impulse, he did something he had never done before. He motioned for Jane to join him on the stage. Somewhat uncertain and bewildered, Jane complied. The audience grew silent as they curiously watched Bob give her a peck on the cheek.

"Ladies and gentlemen," Bob began, "let me explain and introduce to you my dear wife, Jane." When the applause died down, he continued. "I know you're curious why I asked Jane to join me. I'm sure it's quite uncommon during a political campaign speech. I spent much of the day reviewing my presentation for you this evening. I pondered long and hard before coming to the conclusion that most of you have probably known me for years as you watched me during my tenure in the state legislature. You know I'm a fiscal conservative. You know that wasting a single dollar of your hard-earned tax
~~~

money is not acceptable. You know the values and principles I stand for. You know I've never lied to my constituents and never will."

Bob paused. He looked at Jane and drew her closer before scanning the audience again and continuing.

"But ladies and gentlemen, after what happened last night I decided to share with you some very real and important aspects of our lives that you could not have known." Bob put his mouth close to the microphone and quietly said, "Jane and I would not be here if it were not for miracles in our lives." The large auditorium remained utterly silent. "In fact, had it not been for a miracle, Jane and I would never have been husband and wife. Had it not been for miracles, we would never have survived two violent freeway car crashes. While both of those crashes totally demolished our cars, we walked away unharmed.

"Last night I was picked up from another part of the state in a small, single-engine airplane. As we were approaching Olympia for landing, the engine quit. Frantically, the pilot attempted to restart the engine. He succeeded, and we continued our approach. I could already see the runway lights. Only a patch of forest separated us from a safe landing. Then the engine quit again. There was no time and no altitude to attempt a restart. Moments later, we were brushing the treetops. Then a jarring crash, and everything went dark.

"The first thing I saw when my mind cleared was a State Patrol officer bending over me. He asked, 'Sir, where were you sitting in the plane?'

"I was confused. I told him I had been sitting in the passenger seat.

"He motioned toward the wrecked plane some distance away and said, 'There is no passenger seat in the plane.'

"You see, the seat was gone. The plane had run over it after impact, and it now lay many feet away from the wreckage. It seems that when the plane hit the ground, I'd left my seat and found something else inside the plane to hold onto.

Meanwhile, the seat flew out and was destroyed."

Bob stopped briefly. He put his right arm around Jane's waist before going on.

"Ladies and gentlemen, we not only believe in miracles. We have *experienced* miracles in our lives over and over again, and Jane and I share a rock-solid faith in the author of all miracles – our Almighty God." Bob took Jane's hand, and they both pointed their fingers heavenward. Then she left the stage to thunderous applause.

Bob smiled as he prepared to launch into his speech. It was going to be a good night.

The End

"*The Way it Was* is engagingly told as the experiences and feelings of a youth, yet the specter of Nazi occupation is never absent. Would the Germans discover the hidden radio and the pistol that had not been turned in? Would they discover the man they wanted, dead or alive, that the family was hiding? What would happen if they did?"

Cal Bratt, Tribune Editor

"I found *The Way it Was* well written. Very informative and deeply moving."

Neil Chapman
Texas

"*The Way it Was* honors all the men and women who served during WWII. It accurately conveys what it was like, for a young boy, to live in a country occupied by repressive foreign forces. Fear, faith, humor and laughter are woven throughout the book and become one."

J. Prince
Grand Rapids, MI

ORDER YOUR COPY OF THIS AMAZING STORY TODAY!
A FIGHTER PILOT IN BUCHENWALD
Joe Moser's journey from farm boy to fighter pilot
to near starvation in a Nazi concentration camp.

by Joseph F. Moser
as told by Gerald R. Baron